Getting to Work with the Avid S6

This complete guide to the Avid S6 console offers the best techniques and practices from a seasoned industry veteran, Curt Schulkey, for utilizing its unique features and functions.

The Avid S6 was created to be the industry standard virtual mixing console; however, it is so feature-packed that it can be difficult for new users to navigate. This book provides the ultimate guide to breaking down these amazing features and demonstrating how to use them effectively in your next project, with easy-to-follow instructions, rich illustrations, and general real-world advice from the author.

This book takes students from neophyte to high-level intermediate. Readers should begin with a functional knowledge of Pro Tools and general understanding of mixing for cinema, but previous knowledge of mixing surfaces is not necessary as this book provides guidance through rudimentary, basic, and intermediary level workflows.

Curt Schulkey is a post-production industry veteran, and an educator at Loyola Marymount University in Los Angeles. He continues to work as a supervising sound editor, dialogue editor, and mixer on feature films and longform streaming content.

Getting to Work with the Avid S6

An Introduction and Learning Guide

Curt Schulkey

Routledge
Taylor & Francis Group

NEW YORK AND LONDON

First published 2022
by Routledge
605 Third Avenue, New York, NY 10158

and by Routledge
2 Park Square, Milton Park, Abingdon, Oxon, OX14 4RN

Routledge is an imprint of the Taylor & Francis Group, an informa business
© 2022 Curt Schulkey

Library of Congress Cataloging-in-Publication Data
A catalog record for this book has been requested

ISBN: 978-0-367-62999-1 (hbk)
ISBN: 978-0-367-62996-0 (pbk)
ISBN: 978-1-003-11180-1 (ebk)

DOI: 10.4324/9781003111801

Typeset in Arial Nova
by Apex CoVantage, LLC

To my partner, friend, wife, producer, director, and inspiration, Lisa Pegnato.

Contents

Acknowledgments

As much as I would like to say "I did it all myself; nobody helped," that is not true. From the start, Tom Burns, a top mix tech at Sony Studios, offered me enthusiastic encouragement and technical assistance whenever it was needed. Jeremy Davis, also at Sony, contributed his personal expertise and support as well.

Since much of my empirical study of the S6 took place in the Playa del Rey studios of Loyola Marymount University, I have to thank the university at large, and specifically thank Recording Arts Chair, Professor Rodger Pardee for his encouragement, and LMU tech guru Brian Kotowski for his patient assistance. When the pandemic hit, closing LMU's Playa campus completely, Peggy Rajski, Dean of the School of Film and Television, cleared the way to grant me special access to the locked-down facility. When I needed to explore S6 modules which LMU did not own, Trip Brock at Monkeyland Audio generously opened a mix room for me. Thank you all.

I also want to thank editor Katherine Kadian who's sleuthing was instrumental in getting this book to publication. Thanks, too, to Editorial Assistant Alyssa Turner for keeping the whole publishing process under control.

Preface

> People plot and people plan
> their actions and their lives,
> but sometimes things just happen
> on their own, to our surprise.

This book seems to have begun all on its own.

I have been teaching part-time in the School of Film and Television at Loyola Marymount University for the last several years, sneaking out of work a bit early on Thursday nights to fight my way across Los Angeles at rush-hour, usually arriving in time to start my 7:15 class in post-production sound. When LMU decided to vastly expand their SFTV footprint into a slightly off-campus location, I was happy that it shortened my commute by a few miles. Their new facility was nicely equipped with two new rooms which sported Avid S6 mix surfaces, and the paint was still wet behind the doors when classes were to begin.

In my "day job" as supervising sound editor, I had been working in very close proximity to the S6 for the previous few years and had attended a few hands-on orientation sessions when Warner Bros installed their first S6, but most of my real mixing experience was on its predecessor, the ICON D-Control. I had absorbed enough of the S6's functions from watching mixers and chatting with engineers and mix techs, that I could use it at a very basic level, but I was by no means an expert. I was a bit surprised, then, to be asked for advice when faculty users at LMU became perplexed as to why their tracks did not appear on the surface, or why no sound was coming out of the speakers, or other seemingly basic questions. I did not know the answer to their questions, but I poked at the surface and prodded into the documentation, and I discovered a sprawling range of "gotcha's" that could snag the unwary user.

I set about to put together a short instructional paper which would get new users started and maybe keep them going using the S6. I had estimated that 8 to 12 pages would do it. However, I began to find that most problems that people were having were not simple "one-step" fixes; to use the S6 moderately well required a much wider knowledge base than expected.

When my instructional paper hit 80 pages I realized that it had no clear structure, and there were many more elements that I had not yet addressed. It was much too long for a "quick instructional." I determined that this undertaking would require an entire book. I knew that books are supposed to be written by experts on their subjects, but I felt I was in an interesting position of useful ignorance. I was seeing the S6 from the same perspective as other learners, and this might aid me in addressing their needs. They could not use or appreciate the cool features of this device if they couldn't find the power switch. So, I jumped in; reading, interpreting, talking to tech experts, and trying to explain, in an understandable sequence, how to use and love this complicated, fun toy, er, I mean, tool.

I hope this brings understanding, power and confidence to novice S6 users, elevating them to intermediate level and beyond.

Part I
Fundamental Knowledge

Welcome to the S6

Introduction

The Avid S6 is the workhorse virtual mixing desk for cinema, television, and other media, used in film studios, commercial studios, home studios, and schools throughout the world. The S6 was created to be an industry standard virtual mixing console to interface with Pro Tools® and other workstations. Unlike other digital cinema mixing consoles, the S6 acts as an interface, not as a recording device. The S6 is a collection of physical knobs, sliders, buttons, touch screens and other controls. The S6 reads the touches, slides, twists, pushes and adjustments which the mixer makes to those controls and conveys them to the workstation(s). The workstation(s) can write the values into its timeline, and can then play back those adjustments, displaying them on the surface controls and modifying the sounds per those adjustments.

The Avid S6 is designed to be operated by a diverse group of users. It addresses the different needs, workflows, and behaviors of its users by presenting to them many different working options. On the S6 there may be several ways to accomplish a single task; the user may decide which method fits their way of working and thinking. This flexibility, however, adds complexity to the process of learning how you might want to best use this powerful tool.

There are videos and tutorials about this console which demonstrate its many features, and some of them *may* prove to be very helpful to your understanding of the S6. But when I began to try to understand, control and master the S6 myself, I found two significant shortcomings. First, videos demonstrated features as if they were freestanding parts of the whole – with no depth and no real plan to guide me towards an understanding of how to really sit down and work with this tool. Too often they show features which require you to have previously created setups, settings or systems without which the features just do not work. Secondly, videos are linear, with a fixed time of presentation. After watching a 20-minute video on creating layouts, I had an idea of what was possible, but when I got about four steps into doing a task and could not recall the exact sequence of button pushes and menu selection, I found it difficult to jump back to the exact point in a video where I could find the information I needed. With a book you may skim, jump forward or backward, make notes in the margins or look to the index to more quickly remind yourself of the necessary steps, methods, and procedures for accomplishing your desired tasks.

How to Learn

I believe it is easier to learn to use the S6 by starting with the basic usage, then introducing more complex and intricate features.

Some readers will have deep experience and understanding of mixing, and possibly mixing on virtual surfaces. Some readers will be new to the entire world of mixing, control surfaces, and sound-to-picture workflows.

This book will begin from the start, presuming that the reader has no experience with this device. I will try to take you on a reasonable journey of enlightenment. Good luck to all of us.

Chapter 1

Beginning Work on the Avid S6

Starting from Scratch

For new users of the S6, it is difficult to know which skills and tools are basic and essential, which should be learned later, and which should be ignored completely.

The S6 is a complicated device with layers of overlapping functions and nested settings. The positive aspect of this redundancy is that it allows users different paths to accommodate their individual ways of thinking and working. At the start of the digital revolution – when work in the world of audio was transitioning from electro-mechanical tools to computerized, virtual tools – we experienced many different approaches to workstation design and implementation. Most of those workstations allowed only one method to accomplish a task. A fade-in was created, for example, by doing step 1, step 2, and step 3. If the user had the same mindset as the designer, the tool was easy for them to use, while people with different personalities, experiences or characteristics might find it frustrating or impossible. After much pushing and pulling between software designers and users and between competing workstation creators, those tools which had the most versatility attracted the most users. Workstations which offered limited flexibility in workflow lost their place in the market. Digi Design®, the developers of Pro Tools, eventually became the powerhouse of audio workstations, in part due to the flexibility of their products. Now we can create a fade-in with Pro Tools by selecting an end-point and pressing **Ctrl + D**, or by selecting an area at the start of a clip and pressing **Cmd + F**, or by using **Edit > Fades > Create**, or I can drag across the start of a clip with the magic tool, and maybe there are a couple of other ways I never learned to use. There is room for improvement in the S6, but right now it is the best tool available, so let us explore how to use it.

Using the S6 is not always intuitive. There are terms that are used in untraditional ways, buttons, knobs, and switches which have ambiguous or unusual labels, and long lists of settings, options, and modes. It is easy for new users to get stuck – unable to make the console work – simply because they cannot recognize that a setting or mode

DOI: 10.4324/9781003111801-2

needs to be changed, or how to change it. Empirical attempts to divine procedures on this surface can cause users to auger into the mud.

In most commercial settings, there is an experienced mix technician or engineer on hand who helps the mixer find their way on this console. In a school setting, students more often need to work on their own. They therefore need to have a higher level of knowledge about the S6 before they can begin creating mixes effectively.

With this book I am trying to present the first level of required understanding of this device and its operation. At the start I will skip over several complicated features such as Layouts, Spill Zones, Post Module States, Layout Banking positions, VCA masters, etc. because those features will be better understood and utilized after learners are comfortable with the basic operations of the surface. This book will not cover everything there is to learn about the S6. It is not a reference manual. Avid's manual "S6 Guide" is the ultimate reference. New users should study its content and structure as it can be invaluable when seeking information on individual controls or functions.

The S6 is not easily mastered without developing a body of knowledge regarding its operation, and I hope to fill that need. There are several pages of background information which users need to understand before any real work on the surface begins, so please be patient and bear with the instruction. Your experience with the S6 will be much more satisfying, less frustrating, and more time-effective if you take this in steps.

Special Terms or Word Usage

Avid is not always consistent or conventional with its terminology. To alleviate some of the confusion I have compiled a few terms which require some explanation and understanding. It may help you to know their Avid meanings before you get too deeply into the S6.

Process/Function – Avid calls EQ, compression, expansion, and other things which plug-ins do, or even the plug-ins themselves, Processes or Functions. Avid uses the terms interchangeably. This document will use "function" as a noun – except where Avid uses "Process" as an official designation. I will refer to the Process Module as such, since that is what Avid calls it, but all those tools which effect sound, such as EQ's, compressors, or other plug-ins, I will call functions. The things which those functions do to audio, I will call processes.

Control – Any knob, button, switch, or fader is a control. Controls may be physical or virtual. There are many references to controls, so keep in mind that a control is one of those individual items.

Button, knob, switch, fader, etc. – Even though these are controls, they will be referred to by these crude names when appropriate. These are indeed controls, but as individuals, they require more identifiable names. The Avid manual likes to use "key" or "switch" or "encoder" to describe them, but I usually press buttons, twist knobs, flip switches, and slide faders.

Edit – Avid sometimes uses the term *edit* to refer to changing written parameters. I might say that you are using a control to change a setting, whereas Avid might say that you are editing a parameter.

Attention – Avid uses this word as a verb – in place of "bring to attention." You can attention a track. The past-tense "attentioned," which upsets the spellcheck, is used instead of "bringed to attention." After I attention a track, that track is attentioned. If was attentioning my writing I would have used "brought" in that last sentence.

Layout. – Avid uses this word in at least three different ways. Three of them are:
- A Track Layout is a user-defined configuration of tracks from one or more attached workstations. Users can assign tracks from their workstation(s) to a layout in any sequence desired. Once created, a layout may be recalled to the surface. Users can define up to 99 different layouts within one layout set. Track Layout sets may be saved, transferred, and recalled.
- A Display Layout is a factory-designed graphic configuration of meters, waveforms and other data shown on the Display Module at the top-end of the track modules. Users may choose among the seven Display Layouts provided, but those seven layouts cannot be modified. In addition, there are three different Master Meter layouts, also factory-designed, which may be applied to a Master Meter Module.
- A Meter Layout is like a Track Layout. It defines which tracks are displayed in a Master Meter Module. This layout can be built from the tracks of one or more attached workstations, saved and recalled.

Selection. In this book, when "Selection" is capitalized it refers specifically to an area within a workstation track which has been selected. A Selection can be moved, saved, and adjusted. The word is otherwise used as an action noun, as in "When your selection is complete, press **OK**."

Insert – When used as a verb, Avid usually means "place into," as in "Insert a plug-in into a track." This sometimes gets confusing because a plug-in is also an insert. This could lead to: "Insert an insert into a track." I will use "instantiate" to describe the assignment of a plug-in into a track, and "insert" as the noun. "Instantiate an insert into a track" clarifies the action. Sometimes the verb form of insert must be used for other purposes.

Spill Zones – The S6 allows users to designate up to two groups of contiguous channel strips on the surface as areas where selected groups of tracks from workstations can be assigned, or "spilled." The zones are named Left Spill and Right Spill, and smart users designate channel strips on the left side of the surface as the Left Spill, and those on the right as the Right Spill, but the zones may be designated anywhere on the physical surface.

Cut – This is the equivalent to Mute. If a **Cut** button is lit, that element is muted.

In – This is the opposite of Bypass. If the **In** button of a function is lit, it is not bypassed.

Shift Keys – The S6 has three different kinds of Shift keys, sometimes more. These Shift keys usually only affect their own module, the Modifier Shift being the exception. I have improvised some new terms to help distinguish one from the other.

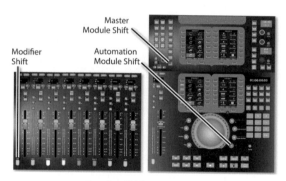

Location of different shift keys

Shift – The first is the Shift key found along the bottom portion of the Fader Module(s). This is a duplicate of the **Shift** key on the workstation keyboard, as are the **Option, Control,** and **Command** keys. With these close-by modifier keys you do not need to stretch to reach the Workstation keyboard. I refer to this key as the **Shift** key or the **Shift** modifier key.

mmShift – (Master Module Shift). This Shift key is on the left side of the Lower Master Module. It operates on some button groups of the Master Module. More advanced users will utilize this key extensively.

amShift – (Automation Module Shift). This Shift key is in the center area of the Automation Module, near the Jog wheel. It operates on Jog wheel functions.

pmShift – (Post Module Shift) This Shift key is on the Post Module (not shown).

jmShift – (Joystick Module Shift) This Shift key is on the Joystick Module (not shown).

Shift Key Helpers – On the Master Modules, the LEDs of buttons that are affected by any modifier key will light when the modifier key is held down. This is a great confirmation that the key will act on the button.

OLED (organic light emitting diode) – The little displays which show text and parameter values all across the S6 are made up of OLEDs and are called OLED displays, but I will shortcut it and simply call the displays OLEDs.

Knob Cluster – Avid sometimes refers to these as Encoder Sections. A Knob Cluster is a grouping of a knob, OLED and some buttons (see "Knob Cluster Behavior" on page 47).

Settings in General

The settings of the S6 can help you or frustrate you. Scrolling through the settings screens can seem random until you understand their structure. (*This is not helped by the fact that some headings within those screens are used more than once across different settings categories.*) Managing the settings will make you a more powerful user.

There are different kinds of saved settings on the S6; System Settings, User Settings (aka User Preferences), and Titles. Custom and Default Soft Key data can also be saved, but that is more of a concern for advanced users.

Many of the settings address the different working approach of each user. One user will find a particular setting useful and another user may find it annoying. When any user sits down at this console, those settings will usually be in the state in which the previous user left them. It is therefore important for you to know what those settings do, how to change them, and how to save and recall groups of settings to the state which *you* find most useful. If you ignore the current settings, you could encounter some interesting surprises.

Types of Settings

System settings are specific to the setup of each S6 system, such as physical layout of the console. System settings are not transferable; they stay with the console. We will explore system settings later in the book, so do not concern yourself too much about them at this time; just know that you will rarely change system settings.

User Preferences affect the operational behaviors of the S6, allowing different options to different users, such as meter Display Layouts, glide times, and spill zone locations. Individual users can save their User Preferences to a removable file so that they may load their personal preferences into the S6 before starting a work session.

Some settings are Title settings. These include Track Layouts, locked strips, banking states and other modes which relate to a specific project (aka title). These settings may be saved to Title files, which are different from other preference files. Title files can be saved to or loaded from the S6 environment or removable media.

The S6 can be configured so that User Preferences and Title files are embedded into, and therefore saved with your Pro Tools session, and then automatically loaded into the S6 when you open the session. *(See "Designate Pro Tools Sessions for automatic preference use" on page 37)*

You Should Control the Settings

You do not need to know all the details of settings but be aware that the settings could have been left in disarray by the last user, or the configuration setting which tells the S6 to automatically load preferences might have been disabled. *The best practice for anyone sitting down to the S6,* is to either check that auto-load is enabled, or to manually load your collection of settings into the console and then proceed. We will go into details on this soon. *(See "User Preferences" page 32)*

Settings for Beginners

To start with clean and neutral settings, begin your work session by loading a default Title and Preference settings. A title file named "**BWA_S6_Default_Title**" and a User Preferences file named "**BWA_S6_User_Prefs**" can be downloaded to a USB drive and loaded into your S6 system. You will learn how to do this when we explore procedures for starting up the S6.

Three Quick Tips
Outboard Keyboard

There is no hardware keyboard built into the S6. Any typing you need to do, such as entering names of preference files, tracks, Layouts, etc. must be done using the software keyboard on the Touchscreen. This is good for most quick entries, and ideal to use when mixing, but if you are building templates or creating well-labeled layouts, it helps to have a hardware keyboard available. This is easily done.

On the back side of the Touchscreen assembly are two USB connectors. Small USB Windows keyboards are cheap and easy to find. It only takes a few seconds to hook one in and type away!

A Most Important Setting

One Pro Tools (not S6) preference must be set in a specific way to prevent users from adversely affecting their projects. In Pro Tools, go to: **Setup > Preferences > Mixing > Setup**, uncheck **Auto Insert Default Plug-Ins from EUCON Surfaces**. When this is checked, pressing some of the selection buttons in the Process section of tracks will insert plug-ins into tracks. The Pro Tools default is **ON**, but this is not desirable in most circumstances. Uncheck it (*for a longwinded explanation of why, see "What's So Bad About Auto Insert?" on page 200*).

Pro Tools setting: Setup > Preferences… > Mixing > Setup

If you open Pro Tools preferences on a system which is not connected to a EUCON® surface, this checkbox will be grayed-out and probably still in the default state, but since this is a system setting, you will need to be sure that the Pro Tools which is running your session for the S6 is properly set.

LEDs Point the Way

The S6 designers implemented a very clever tool which can help you on nearly every module. Whenever a button is poised for action, its LED will light.

Take the Banking buttons as an example. Whenever the banking buttons are focused on a set of tracks which can be banked, their LEDs will light. If tracks are available to the right, the right bank button will light. When tracks are available on the left, the left bank button will light. When no tracks are available to bank, the bank buttons go dark. Keep an eye on this behavior and your personal mixing power will increase.

An Overview of the S6 Surface

You do not need to know how to build a mixing console to find your way on the S6, but you will need to know the names and locations of the sections of the console. S6 consoles may be configured in different ways for different users and needs. They are assembled from a set of standard modules. The configuration is not something you can change easily – it requires unbolting chassis parts and re-routing power and ethernet cables. In most cases users learn to work with the configuration that they have available.

Avid breaks the modules down into two major types: Master Modules and Track Modules.

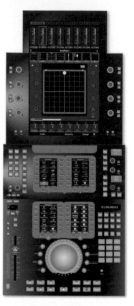

Master Modules

The Master Modules are usually located in the central area of the console. They give global control of specific tasks or modes. Most consoles have only one of each type of Master Module. Master Module types are:

- The Upper Master Module
- The Lower Master Module
- The Automation Module

Two *optional* Master Modules are the Post Module (*see "Introducing the Master Post Module" on page 155*) and the Joystick Module (*see "Introducing the Joystick Module" on page 165*). Many systems do not include these modules. As they are specialty modules, they will be covered later in this book.

Master Modules

Knob Modules and Display Modules, which are part of the normal track module configurations (*see next section*), may be installed and configured as Master Modules as well.

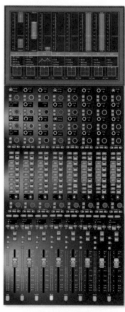

Track Modules

Track Modules consist of sets of eight identical columns of controls which, when stacked above or below one another in the console frame, will form channel strips, columns of controls which operate on a specific track or audio path. Installing additional sets of these modules side-by-side will each add eight tracks to the console's surface capacity.

Track modules consist of:

- Fader Module
- Process Module

Track Modules

- Knob Module
- Display Module (optional)

Additional track modules can be installed in custom configurations in the S6 frame. They can then be used as additional sets of controls, allowing a control path to be directed to them to give users more knobs, buttons and sliders to fool with.

Surface Configurations

The S6 modules *could* be assembled into the frame in any desired sequence. For example, the faders can be installed at the top, far away from the mixer's fingers. That would not be normal for humans. The placement of each module into the S6's frame is called the surface configuration.

Typical surface configurations consist of one Master Module (upper and lower) and one Automation Module in the center, one or two bays of track modules to the left of the Master Modules, and one or two bays of track modules to the right.

This simplified illustration shows only one of each track module.

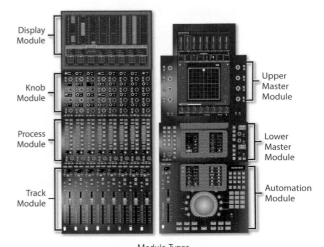

Module Types

Although there are quite a few knobs, buttons, and sliders on the track modules, each channel strip is identical, so you only need to know how one track strip works in order to operate this console effectively.

A Closer Look at the Master Modules

The Master Module is the central control area of the S6. From the Master Module users turn the power on or off, adjust system and project settings, and reach into the computer which is running the console. Sub-modules of the Master Module usually populate this area of the console.

The Master Module is often configured in the center of the console. It consists of an upper and a lower section.

Master Module – Upper Section

The top portion of the Master Module contains the Touchscreen, the **Home** button, and the **Back** (◢▬▬◣) button. On either side of the Touchscreen are four sets of knob clusters called the Attention Track Knobs. We will get to the operation of those knobs later in this book.

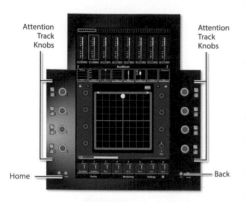

Master Module Upper Section

The Touchscreen is part of the Upper Master Module. Different "screens" displayed on the Touchscreen can give access to different aspects of the S6's settings or operation. Some screens control global attributes, others give a larger representation of fader-strip controls, and some enable creation of custom layouts and other settings.

Main screens of the Touchscreen

There are five primary Master Module screens: **Home**, **Settings**, **Tracks**, **Monitoring**, and **Workstations**. There are sub-sets of those screens. Do not worry about these just yet.

Navigating Around in the Touchscreen

The Home Screen provides a point from which to navigate to other primary screens. To do so, you need to quickly get to the Home screen from whichever screen is being displayed.

Home Screen button

Navigating to the Home Screen

There are other ways to get to the Home Screen, but the simplist way is – *Press the Home button*. This actual button is on the left of the Touchscreen assembly, near the bottom, always available.

We will explore the features available on the Home Screen later, but what you need to know as you begin is that the Home Screen can be a gateway to the other primary screens if you ever need them.

To navigate from the Home Screen to another primary screen, do one of the these:

- Touch the screen name at the very bottom of the Home Screen.
- Touch the Soft Key button below the screen name on the Home Screen.
- Swipe across the Touchscreen until you reach the desired screen.
- Use dedicated **Home**, **Tracks**, **WS** (Workstation), or **Settings** buttons in the Navigation Buttons area of the Lower Master Module *(see Master Module – lower section below)*.

The Touchscreen is a large Windows Tablet. Swipe up or down to scroll within a screen. Swipe left and right to scroll to different pages or screens.

Some screens have a small gear icon in the lower-right corner; the Local Options icon (✿), which calls up options specific to that screen.

Master Module – Lower Section

There is a **Shift** button on this module. It is the Master Module **Shift** button. It is not the same as the Shift key on any keyboard or on the fader module. It modifies the functioning of several buttons on the Master Module, so find this key and remember where it is. It will be referred to in this book as "**mmShift**," although the button just says "**Shift**."

Master Module – lower section

The lower section of the Master Module contains eight Main Menu Buttons which are spread across the top of the Lower Master Module. As the displays on the Touchscreen above them change, the functions of these buttons change. The user may press a button instead of touching the button name that is displayed on the Touchscreen above it. You are more likely to simply touch the button name on the Touchscreen; button presses or Touchscreen touches achieve the same results.

Automation Module

The Lower Master Module contains the Navigation Buttons, an assignable knob[1] (bottom left), and two Soft Key pads with the buttons which select Soft Keys. Along the bottom of each Soft Key pad are Soft Key Navigation Buttons which change the content of the Soft Key displays. Studio/Talk and Monitoring Controls are on the bottom right of this module section.

> I find the identification of "Monitoring Controls" and "Studio/Talk" sections to be perplexing; they seem mis-labeled in the Avid documentation. The area designated as "Studio/Talk" actually controls the monitoring, while the "Monitoring" area controls the studio and talkback. In addition, "Navigation Buttons" have little to do with navigation. To remain consistent with Avid I shall maintain the official names of these areas. Flexibility keeps the mind nimble.

Automation Module

Several helpful tools reside in the inaptly named Automation Module. This Master Module contains the Attention Track Fader, Transport Controls, the Time Code display, a numeric keypad and two additional Soft Key pads. The big wheel in the center is a Jog/Shuttle wheel with its own modifier buttons surrounding it.

Locate Section

The cluster of buttons below the Location display, which Avid calls "Locate Switches," allows users to change the Selections in the workstation and to jump to timeline locations of the workstation session.

---

1. This assignable knob only works with Logic Pro X, Cubase or Nuendo, so ignore it if you are using Pro Tools.

Three very important buttons in this section control the active workstation session; **Save**, **Undo**, and **ReDo**. Any of these buttons will light when there is data in their buffer. To save the current session, you must press **Save** two times quickly.

(If you do not see these keys on your surface, see "Button Name Changes" at the end of this chapter.)

Another interesting button in this area is the **Mem Loc** button. When pressed, the Memory Locations Soft Key Page 1 will be assigned to the right softkey pad in the Automation Module. The Memory Locations page allows you to utilize Pro Tools Memory Locations. This Soft Key page is not persistent; it will disappear when other Softkey Page assignments are made.

Any track in your session can be "attentioned," which mirrors it into the Attention Track Fader, where graphic and colorful knobs and displays are available on the Master Module Touchscreen *(see "Attention Mode" on page 96)*.

The numeric keypad mimics the numeric keypad of the workstation keyboard. Beware that the keys are in a slightly different configuration than most workstation keyboards.

The transport controls give you an easy-to-reach collection of transport controls and some additional buttons to control the Selections within the Pro Tools tracks. The four buttons on the bottom row center are the most useful *(see "Transport Controls and Navigating in the Timeline" page 49)*.

Important Note on Button Name Changes

Many of the S6 consoles out in the real world were delivered with buttons in the Locate section named unconventionally. They were so unconventionally named that Avid changed the names to fit the actual purpose of those buttons. Avid manufactured sets of overlays (stickers) to be placed on some buttons. Inevitably some consoles exist with only the original button names. If you are having trouble locating the Locate buttons mentioned above, here is a translation chart.

Table 1.1 Locate Section Button Changes

Old Button Name	New Button Name
Trim +	Mix/Edit
Trim –	Faders Off
Store Current	Trim Sel
Store Locate	Cons Clip

(Continued)

Table 1.1 (Continued)

Old Button Name	New Button Name
Edit	Mem Loc
Recall	Undo
Delete	Redo
Clear	Save

Interestingly, some of the documentation from Avid still shows the old names.

Chapter 2
Starting the S6 Systems

Turn on and tune in without dropping out.

On a cold morning, start the engine of your car and rev it hard and fast; make it scream! With the accelerator to the floor and a foot hard on the brake, slam it into reverse gear. If it stalls, start it up and rev it harder to back out of the driveway. Keep the parking brake on hard while you rev up again to throw it into drive. Ignore the smoke from the rear wheels; that's probably normal. When you get to your destination, hold the brake hard again, rev hard and shift into reverse and hope the engine stops. If not, pop the hood and yank out spark plug wires one at a time until it quits. Pull off a battery wire to shut it down. Now that's the way to keep your car in tip-top shape.

-Anonymous Porsche Owner

After reading through Chapter 1, you should have absorbed enough information to enable you to *finally* sit down and start-up the Avid S6. It won't be long before you can try out some of those controls.

To keep your S6 systems in tip-top shape, there are some very simple startup and shut-down practices which ensure that you and the machine have a long happy life together.

Follow this protocol every time. Do these in the proper order.

Cut to the Chase: Startup Summary

1. Power-up the S6 if it is not already turned on.
2. Power-up the workstation computer(s).
3. Confirm Link-up with XMon® and WSControl®, or DADman®.

DOI: 10.4324/9781003111801-3

4. Lock XMon to the S-6.
5. Confirm Monitor Selection.
6. Confirm Monitor Level (and **Dim** and **Mute** buttons).
7. Confirm User Preference settings.
8. Open Pro Tools session.

Here is a bit more explanation.

NOTE: Two commonly used monitoring applications are XMon and DADman. Once these have been configured, they will behave in the same way for users. For simplicity, I will refer to them both as XMon.

There are many other monitoring solutions available, some of which bypass many of the monitoring controls of the S6, so some of these instructions may not be relevant to your situation. The studio engineer will be able to advise you regarding your specific installation.

1. The S6 console should be powered-up before starting the workstation.

If the S6 is not already powered-up, you should start it before starting the workstation. Press the large button which is behind the Master Module's touchscreen. It is flat on the console. You will probably need to peek back there to find it. Wait until the S6 is ready, as evidenced by this touchscreen.

2. Start the workstation computer.

The XMon software should auto-start on computer boot-up,[1] and you should see the XMon screen appear on the Mac's screen, like this:

Touchscreen on startup

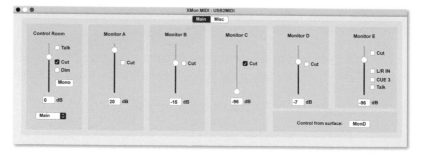

The XMon screen

---

1. Some systems do not utilize any of the Avid monitoring systems, so check with your engineer to confirm that these instructions are relevant to your specific system.

Do not change any of the XMon settings. It is happy the way it is.

If the computer is already running and you do not see the XMon software running – you can restart the computer or start XMon in the Applications folder of the Workstation computer.

An application called WSControl should also auto-start. Its circular icon in the Mac menu bar will spin while it is looking for the S6 on the network. It will stop spinning when it finds the S6. If it is not running, you can restart the computer, or start WSControl in its Applications folder.

WS Control icon

3. Link-up.

The S6 and the workstation computer should be communicating with one-another by now.

At the bottom of the S6 Touchscreen's Home Screen, touch **Settings**, then **Workstations**. You should see the workstation computer's identifier name in the right column, under **Connected**. It should be colored gray.

Workstations screen

If it is red, see "Workstation Not Connecting to the S6 Surface" on page 204.

If the workstation happens to appear only in the left column, under Network, touch-drag the workstation icon from the left column to the right column. *If that does not work, see "Workstation Not Connecting to the S6 Surface" on page 204.*

4. Lock the S6 to XMon.

When other applications are focused on the workstation it is possible for the S6 to disconnect from the XMon application, causing it to lose monitor control. There is a quick way to assure that does not happen.

To lock S6 to XMon

1. Assure that the XMon application is the focused application.
2. In the Control Room section of the Lower Master Module, assure that the upper **Setup** button is lit. If not, press it (*see "Master Module – Lower Section" on page 35*).

5. Set audio monitor selection.

The S6 manages which devices have access to the room speakers, and which speakers are receiving signal. Your system may have several monitoring options, so you should confirm that the monitoring is properly set for what you are trying to hear.

Source Device Selectors

Speaker Selectors

Monitoring screen

Navigate to the Monitoring Screen of the Master Module touchscreen.

The setup of the Monitoring section is dependent on the installation, so you will need to know from your engineers which sources are connected to which Source Device Selector buttons, and which speakers you should be using.

In the top row, select the device which you want to hear. For example, my system is connected like this:

Main = Pro Tools output.
Surround = DVD/ Blu-Ray Player
Stereo 1 = Mac output

The selectors at the bottom of the screen allow users to choose which speakers in the room are on or muted. Generally, they should all be turned on, but your installation may be different. Consult your engineer.

6. Confirm proper monitor level.

Monitor level and muting for the room are set on the Lower Master Module's lower-right side (see "Monitor Levels" on page 24).

- Select **Main Spkrs**.
- The big knob above the **Dim** button sets monitor level. In the illustration it is shown red because the **Cut** (Mute) button is active.
- Adjust Volume knob to "0.0" for your standard reference level. Usually this is 85 dBC, but your system could be set differently.
- **Dim** lowers the level of all speakers by the dim amount.[2]
- **Cut** – Mutes all speakers. Pressing down on the Volume knob will also toggle **Cut**.

---

2. The dim amount is adjusted on the Monitoring Screen's Dim setting.

7. **Check the preference designation or load user preferences and title files.**
   - If you are manually saving and loading Preference and Title files, do so now.
   - If you do not yet know what User and Title setting are or how they work, skip this instruction at this time. You will inherit the settings of the previous user. Do not worry. You will learn about preference designations, User Prefs and Title files in the next chapter. Skip to the next step.
   - If you expect to auto-load and auto-save preferences and Title files, confirm that the desired workstation is designated as auto-load destination. Again, if you do not know what that means yet, do nothing. *(see "Designate Pro Tools Sessions for automatic preference use." page 37).*

Learn more about Preference and Title files at "User Preferences" page 32, and "Title files" on page 32.

8. **Open the Pro Tools or other workstation session.**

Hopefully, all will be happy.

Missing Tracks

If you do not see any tracks on the surface:
1. Check if the LED on the Layout Mode button in the Lower Master Module is lit.
2. If it is lit, press **mmShift** + **Layout Mode** to deactivate Layout Mode.

Layout Mode

mmShift

Navigation buttons

Shutting-Down the S6 Systems

Now that you have the S6 started up, it is time to learn how to safely shut-down the S6.

For the first year or so that I was working on and around the S6, mix techs and mixers would routinely shut-down the console when it behaved erratically. They turned off the power source; literally pulling the plug. If a module misbehaved, the techs would reach into the chassis and pull the power cord out of the socket, then plug it back in. This is just like pulling the plug on any other computer; it is not good procedure. These users routinely had difficulties with erratic behavior of the S6.

The S6 has some built-in tools for correctly re-starting individual modules if they are acting up. I won't be covering that here, but you can find instructions in Avid's S6 Guide. Look for "Utility Test Mode for Modules."

Never power-cycle the S6 by disconnecting power from the running system. It needs to be shut-down using the software processes.

If you are manually saving and loading preferences and Title files, save them before shut-down. Save your User Preferences and/or Title files to a pen drive and load the default files back into the S6. This keeps your changes and leaves the system set correctly for the next user (*see "User Preferences" page 32*).

Always use the following process:

1. Save the Title and preference files (*see "Manually using preference files" on page 35*).
2. Save all workstation sessions, close them, and quit the workstation software.
3. As a courtesy to the next user, load the studio's default Title and preference files (*see "Manually using preference files" on page 35*).
4. Shut-down the workstation computer(s).
5. On Master Module touchscreen, navigate to **Settings** > **About**.
6. At the bottom of the About screen, press **Shutdown**.
   Do not choose **Logout**.

Monitor Levels, Room Mute, and Dim.
What's Happening To Me? ! ? !

Over the years, every now and then I have been sitting peacefully in the mix theater when suddenly, the loudest possible volume level of noise, tones, feedback or random hash came blasting out of the speakers like an explosion, except that these explosions would not end.

When this happens it is very disorienting, and most people duck, cover their ears, and/or run from the room. The best action to take, however, is to mute the room speakers. Once speakers are muted, the cause of the problem can be determined safely. If you are instead running from the room or scrumming about trying to remember where the room Mute button is, you are not caring for yourself, your colleagues, or your clients.

It is an important "health and safety" requirement that you know, in any room where mixing is taking place, how to mute the room speakers.

Using Cut

On standard S6 installations, the speakers are muted by pressing the **Cut** button on the lower section of the Master Module. "Cut" is an alternate word for "mute," and

"Cut" is what the button says. When Cut is lit, the speakers should be off. Pressing down on the Volume knob will also toggle **Cut**.

Your mix room could be wired differently. Check with your mix engineer to learn how to mute and unmute the speakers before you proceed with mixing.

Using Dim

Another health and safety issue is your own possible over-exposure to loud and constant noise levels. The S6 has a wonderful button called **Dim**. When active, **Dim** drops the monitor level of the room by a pre-set amount. I recommend a setting of -10.0 dB to -20.0 dB.

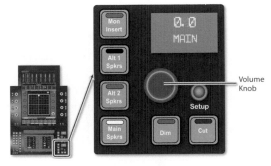

Studio/Talk section

When mixing a loud and complicated sequence, setting the monitor to Dim allows you to hear, explore, pre-set, and work out much of your mixing without fatiguing (or destroying) your hearing. When you go back to mix volume (un-dimmed level) you will have a better understanding of how loud your mix is.

Level

I will not get very technical here, but you need to have respect for the monitor volume setting while you are mixing.

The big knob in the Studio/Talk section usually adjusts the volume of the selected speaker set. If your room is set up correctly, a setting of "0.0" will play sound at the reference level[3] for your room. On many other mix consoles, this control is placed in a less accessible position to avoid accidental or casual level changes. On the S6, it is right there where you might touch it while dimming or muting the speakers.

To avoid mixing at the incorrect monitor level:

- Keep an eye on the setting of your selected room speakers, usually "Main." It should usually be set to "0.0."

---

3. In most cases this will be 85 dB, but some smaller rooms are adjusted lower.

- Never use the monitor level knob to casually turn down the volume in the room. If you want to turn off the speakers, use the **Mute** button (or press down on the Volume knob). If you want to turn the level down for any reason, use the **Dim** button.
- Never *turn* the volume down all the way. Use the **Cut** button instead. Most users are not expecting the volume knob to be turned down, and when they cannot hear the system output, they will waste time looking elsewhere. When they find out what you have done, they will hate you.

To adjust the Dim Amount:

1. On the Touchscreen, navigate to the Monitoring screen.
2. In the right-hand column is a knob marked **Dim**.
3. Adjust the Dim amount using the Attention Track Knob on the side of the Touchscreen. and Keyboard

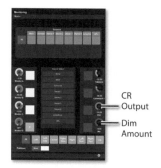

CR Output
Dim Amount

Monitoring Screen level adjustments

Chapter 3

Mixing with Mouse and Keyboard

How To Mix Without Knowing How To Use the Surface

I wish to believe that most of you are reading this book to learn how to use the S6 surface as their primary tool for mixing. If that describes you, then please skip ahead to the next chapter, as this section is intended for those who only want to use their DAW for mixing but need to do so safely and effectively in mix rooms which are equipped with an S6.

It is quite possible to stop right here and use the S6 only as a monitoring system, mixing your project with mouse and keyboard exclusively in the Workstation screen. Since you have started up properly and know that the monitoring levels and configurations are set correctly, you need not touch the surface at all. Mix your project, play it back, record it in the session, or bounce it online or offline, listen to the finished stems or Print Master, and you are done.

This is a rather tragic waste of a powerful and expensive resource, but if you are already facile and effective with your workstation software, and the mouse and keyboard are accessible in the installation that you are using, you will not need to waste all that time learning something new. I have worked on several feature films mixed by Academy Award winning mixers who did not touch the faders or other controls. Instead, they used the mouse and keyboard to accomplish all the mixing adjustments. If you and your film-makers have the time and patience to make one adjustment at a time, I will offer a few suggestions which may enable you to get some value out of the S6.

You *could* skip the rest of this book, but you will miss out on the opportunity to learn to mix on a world-class mixing surface.

DOI: 10.4324/9781003111801-4

No matter what your mixing method is, it is critical that you understand how automation works in Pro Tools. This subject is not covered in this book, but you need to use automation correctly or you risk disaster.

If you do not understand enabling of automation, anchoring of automation, automation breakpoints, automation lanes, automation writing modes, automation type enabling/disabling, trim mode and its consolidation or track-to-track copying/pasting of automation, you need to study up on them. It would be a bonus for your time and effort to learn how to effectively use **Preview**, **Suspend Preview**, **Punch Preview**, and the **Write to...** options.

How to Not Use the Surface
Do Not Watch What You're Doing!

When mixing with only the mouse and keyboard and the workstation software, be it Pro Tools, Logic, or whatever, you should ignore what is happening on the surface itself. The faders may or may not mirror the tracks in your workstation session because the surface could be set to a track mode which is excluding your tracks. You may be bewildered by what the surface is doing. Ignore it – just do not touch it.

A Need for Metering

Although many mixers tell me that they rarely look at the meters as they work, I do not think they are being completely candid. Meters are extremely useful advisors to you in keeping your mix consistent. They can also indicate when things may be going awry, not just the levels, but audio flow errors and other anomalies. For example, while listening to the composite mix, if any audio paths are assigned to the wrong stem, they may not sound different enough for you to notice. But if you see dialog levels bouncing about in the effects stem meter, you will know that something is amiss.

To create meters within Pro Tools you can simply open the Track Output Windows of tracks which you want monitor. These are small and they tend to clutter up the edit or mix window, but they show you what you need to see. However, since you have this expensive console, why not take advantage of some nice built-in meter options.

If you are not touching the fader strips, you can hijack some strips and use their display section to show output meters, giving you a powerful view of the mix that you are creating.

We will soon investigate some easy metering options which allow beginning users to utilize S6 meters. Later, after mastering some intermediate functions of the console, we will attack the more interesting metering possibilities.

Session Design

For most cinema mixing projects, we route audio through our mixing tools to create at least three stems; Dialog (Dx), Music (Mx) and Sound Effects (Fx). The final mix is the combination of those three stems and is usually referred to as the Print Master. It is helpful to have meters which show the output levels of each of the stems as well as the level of the Print Master. It is important for the mixer to see the output levels of the metered tracks rather than input levels. At some point we may want to adjust the level of an entire stem or the entire mix, and we want the meters to reflect those adjustments.

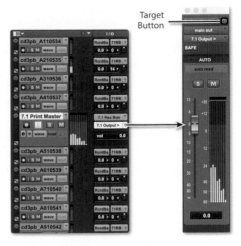

Target Button

Pro Tools: Track Output window

The audio flow structure of the mixing session must lead from tracks, to stem submasters, to Print Master. Generally (though not always) we monitor the Print Master track since that is our final output goal.

The meters which we want to see on the console are: Dx stem, Mx stem, Fx stem and Print Master. The stems can be seen on their own aux tracks (sub-masters) and the Print Master on the Master track of the workstation.

Quckie Meters (This is my pet name, not an official name.)

It is not difficult to get the sub-master and master tracks onto the S6's Display Module of your choice. To use Quickie Meters, decide which channel strips of the S6 you would like use for meter displays.

To Get Meters onto the Display Module.

1. In the Pro Tools session, configure the sub-master and master tracks into contiguous tracks in the sequence you want them displayed.
2. If the channel strips of the S6 are not showing on the surface, see "Missing Tracks" on page 23.
3. Using the **User 1** or **User 2** keys at the bottom of any fader module, bank the console until the master tracks occupy the desired channel strips.

Banking keys

If it helps, you can create empty tracks in the Pro Tools session to act as separators.

Set the Display Layout of each track to something big, like Large Meters.

- Press Attention button (△)+**Select** on each channel strip to cycle through the seven Meter Layouts. Pick layouts that look helpful to you.

The meter format will conform to the track format (i.e., Stereo or 5.1). The meter type and metering settings are selected in the workstation. For more information on how to set meter ballistics, see "Set the Standard" on page 78.

Using the Transport Controls

You may find it helpful to utilize the transport controls rather than the Workstation keyboard. For much more on that, peek ahead to "Transport Controls and Navigating in the Timeline" on page 49.

With that, you may ignore the expensive console and mix with the same tools available to you on your laptop. The advantage will be that you (hopefully) are in a calibrated and engineered listening environment, and you have more useful meters.

Chapter 4

Setting Up the Settings

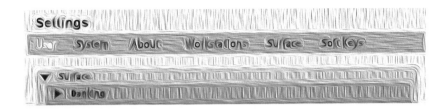

Getting Set

I would love to dig right in and grab some of those knobs and buttons and start driving. We will get to that soon, but experience tells me that understanding a few more concepts and techniques will save you torment and confusion. Adjust the mirrors, check the parking brake, fuel levels, fluid levels, find where the windshield wiper and headlight switches are, and adjust the seat. It is harder to do these things once you are on the highway.

Prepare to Mix! – Preferences and Other Settings

If you want to work effectively on the S6, you must take charge of its preferences and settings.

We will cover User Preferences and Titles, or what might be called personal and project settings. These settings may be loaded from or saved to the S6 system hard drive, a USB drive, the S6 may be configured to automatically load from and save to a Pro Tools (or other workstation) session.

A third type of settings, Soft Key Page Maps, will not be covered. If you get far enough into the S6 surface that you want to use custom Soft Key pages, you will not need this book. Look for it in Avid's S6 Guide.

The Importance of Saving Settings

If you are the exclusive user of an individual S6 and every project you work on is set up exactly the same way, then saving or changing settings may not be important to you. Your settings will remain set.

DOI: 10.4324/9781003111801-5

But if you share the console with other mixers, or if different projects require different set-ups, or if some settings are inadvertently altered, the need changes.

There are many reasons to save and recall collections of your personal and project settings. Other users of a console may change one or many settings, some of which may annoy or stymie you. It is easy to forget how to change a setting that you have not changed recently, which would require searching or researching to find. It never looks good to a client if you are scrolling through lists on the screen or pages on the Soft Key pads, trying to remember how to turn a feature on or off.

If you have developed an efficient way of working with a collection of settings, you can easily bring them along with you if you need to move your work to a different S6 console.

Different projects have different needs, so attaching project-specific settings may make switching from one project to another more efficient.

It is good practice to save your own settings and load them into the S6 at the start of each work session. As a matter of common courtesy, if other individuals are using the S6 between now and when you next use it, you should leave the console with your studio's default settings loaded.

System Settings

What Are System Settings?

These are settings that address a particular S6 installation. They are not designed to be moved from one S6 to another.

System Settings include console configuration, assignment of spill zones, Master Meter Modules, Expand Knob Modules, LED brightness, etc.

Generally, you will not be changing System Settings very often, but you will see some of them in the settings screens.

User Preferences

What are User Preferences?

User Preferences are those settings which you may change that tell the surface how you prefer it to behave. Some of these settings, such as surface brightness, are exclusive to the S6, while others, such as Solo Summing, cross over into the Pro Tools realm as well.

These "crossover" settings may be adjusted in either Pro Tools or the S6, and changes are applied immediately. I have noticed, however, that after changing a setting in Pro Tools, the display in the S6 settings pages does not always update immediately.

One exception to this "crossover" is in Solo behavior, which since version 19 has had an option to give the DAW precedence over the S6. (See **Settings > User > Surface > Strips > Solo Switch**).

Read through the menu beginning on page 215 for a complete list of User Preferences that you can change.

Title Files
What Are Title Files?

Title Files, aka Titles or Title Settings, are collections of settings which can be saved to or loaded from a file. Titles can be configured to include any of these user or system setting types:

- User Preferences
- Banking/Layout State
- Layouts and Meters
- Spill Zone State
- Layout Banked Position
- Expand Faders
- Post Module State
- Post Layouts
- Locked Strips State

FYI – The choice of which of the above elements are included in a Title file is made in the System Settings. This seems a bit confusing at first, but if you were to put this setting among the User Preferences, it would be recursive. Just be aware that if you move from one system to another, you need to check this important setting. Go to **Settings > System > Preferences/Auto-Load from Titles and Sessions** to make your selections.

Once saved, Title Files allow the user to quickly recall (load) a desired group of settings, creating an environment on the S6 tailored to a project (title). *If I had named this setting, I would have named it Project Settings, but nobody asked me to name it.*

User Preferences can be included in the Title Files, or saved and loaded independently of the Title Files, creating the possibility for different individuals to load their own personal preferences, but sharing the rest of the project-based settings via the Title Files.

The Relationship of Title Settings to User Preferences

Title settings may be configured to contain user preference settings.

- Loading a Title file which contains User Preferences will overwrite the active User Preferences on the S6.
- Loading User Preferences after loading a Title file will overwrite the active User Preferences which had been included in the Title file.
- Saving a Title can save the active User Preferences in the Title File along with other Title data.
- Saving the User Preferences will save the currently active User Preferences to a User Preferences file but will not affect other saved files.

To configure which settings are saved within a Title File:

1. On the Touchscreen, navigate to **Settings** > **System** > **General** > **Preferences**.
2. To include User Preferences with the Title, check its box.

Saving and Loading Preferences
Manually or Automatically? How About Both?

Once you have determined which settings to include in your Titles, you may decide if you want your preferences to be stored automatically with the DAW session, or if you want to save preferences manually. Many users do both.

Embedded (Automatic Save and Load)
Pros

- By embedding your preferences into the DAW session of a project, they are automatically saved whenever a session is saved, and automatically loaded when the session is loaded.

Cons

- In situations where multiple users are working in the same session, other users may alter or overwrite your settings.

- DAW sessions can be volatile and may become damaged, particularly when sessions are being worked on in different ways by other team members (possibly on different software versions).
- Mixers will often alter some preferences as they work – honing and adjusting as the project matures. If a project includes multiple sessions, such as a multi-reel feature film, the preferences in those sessions may become different from one-another.

My best mix-tech expert informants advise you to *always* keep a backup copy of your User Prefs and Title Files on an outboard USB pen drive. DO NOT rely on them being saved in a DAW session, as those sessions can be compromised. Keep a second copy. It does not take much time.

Stand-Alone (Manual Save and Load)
Pros
- Saving settings to stand-alone files allows users to maintain safety copies.
- When settings are saved to and loaded from a single file, they will remain consistent across a project. If changes are made during a work session, those changes become incorporated into the stand-alone settings file. (This could be a "con" in some circumstances.)
- Sharing workstation sessions among different team members will not delete settings files.

Cons
- Users may forget to load or save settings files.
- Users may save to or load from the wrong files.

One successful workflow is to do both, save automatically and manually.

Configure the system to automatically save preferences to the workstation session, but also create stand-alone Title and User Preference files. If you change the preferences during a work session, re-save those stand-alone files.

Manually Using Preference Files
Preferences and Titles may be saved onto the system drive of the S6 or on a Windows-formatted[1] drive, usually a USB pen drive.

---

1. Because the S6 is driven by a Windows 10 computer, USB drives must be formatted FAT32 .

Beware! If you save a file to the S6's hard drive, you will not be able to delete that file unless you have access to the Administrator's login on the S6's windows computer, so do not give it a name that you might later regret.

To use a USB drive to store or recall settings files:

- Plug a properly formatted USB drive into the USB port behind the Touchscreen.

There are two USB ports on the back of the Master Module!

To manually save or load a title to or from a file:

1. Navigate to the Tracks page of the Touchscreen. (Shortcut: **mmShift + Tracks** on the Master Module.)
2. Touch **Save** or **Load**.
3. To use a Title file from the S6's system drive
   a. Touch the file name in the displayed list.
   b. Touch **Open** or **Save** in the dialog box.
   c. Skip the rest of these instructions.
4. To use a Title file from a USB drive, in Windows Explorer, navigate to the USB drive.
   - To save, name the file in the dialog box and touch **Save** in the dialog box.
   - To load, touch the desired title file and touch **Open** in the dialog box.

To manually save or load User Preferences to or from a file:

1. Navigate to **Settings > User** on the Touchscreen. (Shortcut: **mmShift + Settings** on the Master Module.)
2. Touch **Save** or **Load** at the bottom of the Touchscreen.
3. To use a User Preferences file on the S6's system drive:
   a. Touch the file name in the displayed list.
   b. Touch **Open** or **Save** in the dialog box.
   c. Skip the rest of these instructions.
4. To use a User Preferences file on a USB drive:
   a. Navigate the Windows Explorer to your USB drive.
   - To save, name the file in the dialog box and touch **Save** in the dialog box.
   - To load, touch the desired preference file and touch **Open** in the dialog box.

Automatically Using Preference Files

Designate Pro Tools Sessions for Automatic Preference Use

Because the S6 has the capability to control more than one workstation, you must designate which application on which workstation will be used to contain the preferences, even if you only have one workstation connected to your S6.

There are two methods for making this designation; use the Touchscreen or use the Soft Key pads.

To use the Touchscreen to designate the target application:

1. On the Touchscreen, navigate to the **Workstation** page. (**mmShift + WS**)
2. Find the desired application in the Applications list.
3. If a little blue star (★) is not visible next to the application (i.e., Pro Tools), touch the space to the right of the application name. The blue star should appear. The blue star indicates that this application has been "designated" for settings to be saved to it and loaded from when sessions are opened or saved.
4. Be sure that the star is next to your DAW application, not XMon, Word, or Gigglebug's Face Race.

Workstations screen

To use a Soft Key pad to designate the target application:

1. Press the **WS** button on the Lower Master Module.
2. On the Applications Soft Key page, press the Soft Key button next to the application to toggle its designation.

A blue star (★) will indicate when an application is designated.

WS Applications page

Note: To designate a DAW application as a target, the application must be running with the S6 successfully connected to that workstation.

Changing Settings

You have read through an awful lot of pages about loading and saving the precious settings, but how do you go about changing them? It is not difficult.

Navigate to the Settings page by doing one of these:

- Press the **Home** button on the Upper Master Module, then one of the following:
  ○ Press the **Settings** Soft Key on the bottom of the Home screen.

○ Touch the **Settings** selection on the bottom of the Home screen.
○ Swipe the Touchscreen pages until you reach the Settings page.
• Press the **Settings** button on the Lower Master Module Locations area.

To navigate to a setting type do one of these:

• Touch one of the type labels at the top of the Settings page.
• Swipe to find the desired screen.

Once the type is found, swipe down to scroll through all settings of that type.

Find the Settings Type That You Need

Settings are split into six groups: `System`, `User`, `Workstations`, `Surface`, `Soft Keys`, and `About`.

Only `System` and `User` are strictly preferences.

`System` and `User` tabs open their respective lists of settings.

`Surface` will open the Surface Configuration and Diagnostic window.

`Workstations` opens the Workstations Screen, the same as pressing **WS** on the Lower Master Module.

`Soft Keys` tab opens the Soft Keys Editor screen, where custom Soft Key pages can be created or edited.

`About` tab gives information about the system and software, and allows Log Out or Shutdown of the S6 system.

For details on these, look to Avid's S6 Guide for your version, or see the listings of settings beginning on page 213. As you find your personal style and methods of mixing, you will be digging into many of them.

Save Or Do Not Save...

After changing a setting, you should consider whether you want that setting saved or not. If you have activated auto-saving of preferences to the Title file or to the Pro Tools session, the change will happen when you save those files, otherwise you must manually save settings to a settings file. If you do not, they will be lost at the next log-out, re-start, or crash of the S6 system.

Chapter 5
The Channel Strip

Mixing Like an Old-School Mixer

By "Old-School Mixer" (OSM) I mean one of those people who does not pay attention to the source of the sound. The sound is coming in through wires in "back room," and if it stops playing, it is someone else's job to find out why and fix it. The OSM does not pay attention to the wires or cords, the mechanicals or the electronics. The OSM sits at the mix desk with hands near the faders and listens to the mix that is being made. They determine what should be loud or quiet. They determine when the balances are right; when something is too dynamic or too flat, too sharp or too dull. They listen, stop and back up a bit, play forward and adjust controls as they go. Mixing like that requires the mixer to think far more about what they are hearing than what their hands are doing, which lights are flashing, or how many tracks are grouped together.

When I work with an OSM, I know that a good part of their intellect *is* controlling those non-creative details, but the mixer has become so practiced with the mix tools that, like a violinist, their creative intellect is transmitted to the fingers without much conscious thought. One difference between an OSM and a violinist is that the operation of the violin hasn't changed much in centuries, but the software of a mix console changes three times a year.

Enough of that. It is finally time to visit the mixing surface for some real button pushing and slider sliding. Yay!

What Are All Those Buttons?

Rather than look at the whole surface and freak out at its awesome complexity, you need only look at one track's channel strip and understand what the controls do.

A channel strip

DOI: 10.4324/9781003111801-6

While the S6 can appear daunting, basic simple mixing is not so very difficult.

So – the best place to start mixing like an OSM is with the channel strips. Let's get a quick look at the different parts of the channel strip, then at banking, then we can look at details of how to use those controls.

A channel strip is one of the eight columns containing sections of each of the four Track modules. You will not be thinking about working with Track modules so much as you will be working with Channel strips; one strip controls one track of audio. The channel strip has different sections, corresponding to the track modules in which those sections reside.

We will begin at the bottom, closest to the mixer' body.

Modifier Keys

The set of eight buttons across the bottom of each fader module are the Modifier keys.

These keys are the color of the current workstation track. Other than color, these keys do not relate directly to the eight tracks of their fader module. They allow the user to enter keyboard modifiers without reaching for a keyboard. I will refer to them as keys instead of buttons because they act as keyboard keys.

Modifier keys (truncated illustration)

The first four are **Shift**, **Ctrl**, **Opt/Win**, and ⌘/ **Alt**; the standard Modifier keys found on computer keyboards. **User 1** and **User 2** keys usually function as Banking buttons.

The last two keys, **Cancel**, and **OK**, will flash whenever a dialog box is active on a workstation screen. They also allow the user to select "**Cancel**" or "**OK**" on the dialog box that is open on an attached DAW.

The Fader Section

The controls of the fader section allow mixers to adjust volume levels, change automation mode, solo, mute, and attention the track. The OLED gives immediate information about the state of the channel.

The Fader

The Fader changes volume for the audio track. It is motorized and touch-sensitive. Up is louder; down is quieter. While the fader is being touched, the volume setting may be displayed in the OLED, depending on user preferences.

The fader can be "flipped" so that it controls some other function in the track, such as a send.

> Flip mode looks great for video demos and sales talks, but I have never seen a mixer using it in real life. It is fun to play with the idea of it, after which you may ignore the feature.

Fader Meters

To the left of each fader are three small strips of LEDs. These strips comprise four context-sensitive tools: input metering, gain-reduction metering, trim match metering, and automation match level. We will get into the details of these much later, but for now, be aware that the left-most strip usually shows input metering.

Fader section

Input Meter

By default, this strip will show the level of signal coming into that channel strip.[1] Because this meter shows input it is not affected by the fader setting; it only shows you that a signal is present in that track. Regardless of the post-fader output, this meter will flash if a signal is present. Just because a signal is showing on this meter does not mean that you should be hearing it. It only shows that there is audio present in this track.

OLED

The fader section OLED displays the track name, automation mode, button function indicators, and Trim and writing modes. Optionally it may show workstation and track numbers. When the fader is touched, the OLED can momentarily display the volume setting. When in Flip mode, it shows the name of the parameter that the fader is controlling. The OLED has some

Fader section OLED

---

1. Meters can be changed to show post-fader levels in Pro Tools menu **Options > Pre-Fader Metering**.

other informational tasks which will be revealed soon. (*See "Changing OLED display options" on page 198*)

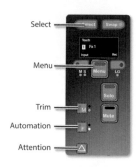

Select

Menu

Trim

Automation

Attention

Fader section buttons

Select Button

The Select button selects the track, just the same as clicking on a track header on the Pro Tools screen. It has other Modifier-key functions as well, such as changing Display Layout for a track.

To select multiple contiguous tracks:

1. Press **Select** on the first track.
2. Press **Shift** + **Select** on the last track. (Use the Shift key on the Modifier keys or the DAW keyboard.)

To select multiple non-contiguous tracks:

1. Press **Select** on a track.
2. Press **Command + Select** on additional tracks.

It may be easier to select tracks on the DAW screen, but this selection method keeps you in front of the faders.

The Attention button (△) assigns (attentions) this track to the Attention Track Fader in the Automation Module. The button lights magenta when active. (*See "Attention Mode" on page 96*)

Attention

Only one track can be attentioned at a time. Attentioning another track or pressing the Attention button again will remove the track from Attention mode.

The Automation Mode button (F) cycles the track through automation modes, displayed on the OLED. If the transport is running, `write`

Automation Mode

mode is skipped for your safety. F lights red when automation is armed, such as with Latch Prime, and it flashes red when automation is being written on this track. When writing automation in Latch mode, pressing F will punch the track out of automation writing. *Why 'F?' An Avid mystery.*

Trim

The Trim button (M) toggles Automation Trim mode on or off. It lights red when writing Trim automation. The word "Trim" will display in a track's OLED when Trim is active. *Why 'M?' Maybe triM?*

The Solo and Mute buttons work as they do everywhere. The behavior of the solo buttons may be set in the DAW application, or in the S6 at Settings > User > Surface > Strips > Solo Switch.

The Menu button can be ignored at this time, but it will not be ignored later. In an ordinary track it does nothing. When using VCA Masters and other track modes, the **Menu** button acts as a Modifier key or special function key. You can do a lot of mixing without using this button. *The name does not give much guidance about this button's usage.*

Top of fader section

The Input and Record buttons flanking the **Menu** button allow you to toggle the state of Input or Record, indicated in the OLED above them. You may find it easier to make these changes in the Pro Tools screen. These buttons sometimes have other jobs. The labels in the OLED above them will indicate their current job.

M, S, LG LEDs

Below the **Input** and **Record** buttons are some indicator LEDs which may mislead you to believe they are associated with the buttons above them. They are not.

- The **M** LED indicates that this track is a VCA Master.
- The **S** LED indicates that this track is a VCA group member.
- The **LG** LED indicates that this track is a member of an active Mix or Edit.

(See "VCA's and How They Started" on page 85 for more details.)

I'm Flipping Out!

One feature of the S6 which could cause you trouble if it is used accidentally is called **Flip to Faders**.

Flip to Faders allows users to swap any parameter control on the surface with the physical fader. For example, you could swap the pan knob with the fader so that the fader now controls the pan setting of its track (and vice-versa). Slide up to pan left, down to pan right. That does not sound helpful to me.

To Flip parameters, press the **Flip** button on the Master Module repeatedly until the desired parameter is assigned to the fader.

To un-flip parameters and return to the "normal" configuration, press **mmShift + Flip** on the Master Module. Spilling tracks or enabling Expand on a track will also un-flip a channel strip, but we have not covered those yet. We will.

The Knob Section

Some S6's are configured with the Knob Modules installed above the Process Modules. Some are configured the other way round because the Knob Section is used more frequently during a mix than the Process section. Either way, I think it helps to know the purpose of the Knob Section before encountering the Process Section.

The Knob Section is a set of knobs which adjust parameters of functions which have been assigned there by the Process Section.

Each Knob Section has four knob clusters comprised of a knob (duh!), two switches (**Sel** and **In**), and an OLED above them.

Note that each OLED references the knob below it. This layout takes some getting used-to, as the OLED appears closer to the knob above it. Or maybe that's just my perception of it.

Three buttons at the bottom allow you to navigate (nudge) through the parameters of an assigned function.

Knob Section

The Process Section

The Process Section is primarily the assignment switchboard for the Knob Module. The Process Module has other functions as well.

From the Process Section, the user controls which functions the knobs of the Knob Section control. The Process Section is the selector of processes. If I were naming it, I would call this the Selector Section, or the Knob Switcher or the Switch-Genie, but Avid did not consult me. So we will stick with "Process Section."

From the Process Section, controls and function parameters may be reset to their factory defaults (see "Bonus Techniques on page 75).

In addition to assigning and resetting functions, the Process Section allows users to change the Bypass state of process types. More details on that will follow (see "Using the Process Section" on page 60).

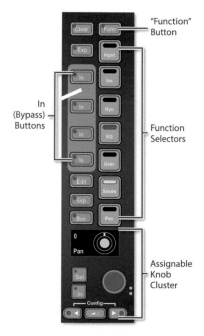

Process section

At the bottom of the Process Section is a customizable knob cluster of its own. By default, this knob controls the L/R pan of the track.

Avoiding Trouble in the Process Section

There is a feature of the Process Section which can cause plug-ins to automatically instantiate into tracks by touching buttons on the Process Section. You are advised to change your settings to avoid creating problems for yourself *(see "A Most Important Setting" on page 11)*.

Although you may set and instantiate Inputs, Busses, and Groups from the Process Section, it is much more easily done on the workstation screen.

By default, front pans are assigned to the "assignable knob," which is helpful.

Surround pans are better controlled in the Attention Track or, if present, in a Joystick Module. The Process Section is best suited to assigning Processes to the Knob Section.

The Display Section

The Display section at the top end of a channel strip is a high-definition display that shows one of seven configurations of meters, waveforms, functions, automation paths and I/O. These configurations are called Display Layouts *(see "Using the Display Section" on page 68)*.

Display section

There are no buttons, knobs, or other controls on the Display section, but it is *the* window into your mix.

The Channel Strip, then, is one area of the surface where the user has access to, and control of, all the processing of sounds in your project. The S6 has a few features which make control of these processes even more understandable and more accessible, so do not stop learning just yet.

Part II

Basic Tools for Mixing

Chapter 6

Basic Tools and Modes

Finally, we shall explore in detail the tools and modes of actual mixing. This chapter is pretty thick, so fire up the mixer and let's begin.

Transport Controls

Many systems I see in studios do not utilize the S6's built-in Transport Controls, so check with your engineer.

The standard S6 Transport Controls at first seem to be self-evident – until you look more closely.

This group of buttons does control the transport with **Play**, **Stop**, **Fast Forward**, and **Fast Reverse** although their arrangement requires some learning. The jump buttons could also be considered transport, and they too are arranged in a challenging configuration. The rest of the buttons do not really belong in the "Transport" category, but here they are, and you may need some of them.

I would advise beginners to restrict their hands to select keys on the bottom row and ignore the meta-keys. Especially – keep your fingers away from the top-left button – which jumps you back to the start of the session. Jumping back to start of session will throw off your mixing rhythm.

> Anyone not confused by this matrix of keys and key combinations just does not understand the situation. Fourteen of these button presses are not transport commands at all. These are a lot of different functions to attach to "transport" keys.
>
> The basic bottom-row keys are not necessarily in a good sequence. A few of these keys will jump your location to somewhere far away, which never makes you look good in front of a client.
>
> These Transport Controls take some getting used to

DOI: 10.4324/9781003111801-8

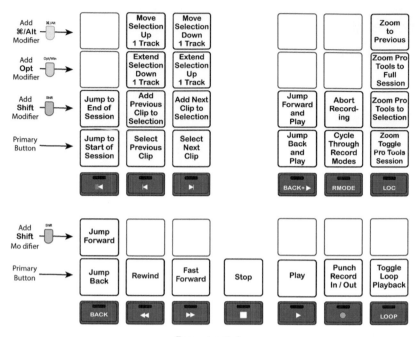

Transport controls

As you can see, some of the modifier combinations have no function. These keys can be customized to execute your personal command set, so if you are into that sort of thing, see "There is another" on page 203.

Navigating in the Timeline
Getting Where You Want To Go

While the Transport Controls offer methods for "playing" the system, we sometimes need to move instantly to a location. You may want to jump onto the Workstation screen and find a location, but there are ways to navigate the session from the S6 surface.

Table 6.1 "Transport" Controls

Button	Function	+ Modifier Key shift	+ Modifier Key Option	+ Modifier Key ⌘/Alt
▶	Play			
■	Stop			
◀◀	Rewind (Hold to roll reverse)			
▶▶	Fast Forward (Hold to roll forward)			
Back	Jump Back 5 seconds	Jump Forward 5 seconds[1]		
Back +▶	Jump Back 5 seconds and Play	Jump Forward 5 seconds and Play		
⏮	Jump To Beginning of Session	Jump To End of Session		
Loop	Toggles Loop Playback			
●	Record. Toggles audio recording.			
R Mode	Cycles the Audio Recording Modes: • Destructive • Quickpunch • TrackPunch • Destructive Punch	Stops or Aborts Record (Depends on Recording Mode Setting)		
Loc	Zoom Toggle (Same as **a...z E**)	Zoom to Selection	Zoom to Session	Zoom Previous
◀	Select Previous Clip in Selected Track(s)	Add to Selection in Selected tracks(s)	Extends Selection down one track[2]	Moves Selection up one track
▶	Select Next Clip in Selected Track(s)	Add Next Clip to Selection in Selected Track(s)	Extends Selection up one track	Moves Selection down one track

---

1. The amount of time jumped is set in Pro Tools – **Preferences > Operation > Back/Forward Amount**.
2. This is counter-intuitive, but true (see *"To move the Selection" on page 183.*).

Caption: The Star button

To locate to a point in the timeline:

1. Press the Star button (★) above the numeric keypad.
2. Key in the Timecode or Feet+Frames position on the numeric keypad (depending on current settings of the workstation).
3. Press Enter on the numeric keypad.

To roll forward or backward quickly do one of these:

• Hold the ◄◄ or ►► button on the Transport Controls.
• Press **Jog** on the Jog Wheel control, then turn the wheel in the desired direction of travel. The farther you turn, the *further* it goes.
• Press **Shuttle** on the Jog Wheel control then turn the wheel. The farther you turn, the *faster* it goes.

Special Note: To use the Jog Wheel to Jog or Shuttle, you must enter `Jog` or `Shuttle` mode, by pressing their buttons next to the Jog Wheel. Their LED will light, indicating that you are in that mode. *While in either mode, many other commands on the S6 do not work as expected*, so it is important to de-activate Jog or Shuttle when you are not using them.

To jump backward or forward by the "Back/Forward Amount."

• On the Transport keys, press **Back** to jump backward.
• On the Transport keys, press **Shift + Back** to jump forward.

Whenever you use the **Back** button in the Transport controls, be careful not to accidentally press the **Jump to Beginning** button, which is just above it.

To Nudge Forward or Backward, by the Pro Tools Nudge Amount:

• Press **+** or **–** above the numeric keypad to move each direction.

Surface Modes

Getting your tracks onto the surface.

To mix your tracks using the channel strips, you need to get those tracks onto the surface. Several modes are available to help you quickly place them within your reach.

Spill zones, VCA Spilling, and Track Layouts offer different ways to direct tracks to the surface, but we will begin with the most basic, Banking mode.

In this mode, the channel strips of the S6 are directly populated with the tracks in the focused workstation (i.e., Pro Tools). When there are more tracks in the session than there are channel strips on the surface, some of those tracks will overflow the surface. If you want to touch a control for a particular track, you may need to slide the surface over (bank it) to expose that track.

Get into Banking

To work in basic Banking mode, you must be able to set the S6 to be *in* Banking mode.

If any LEDs are lit on the **Layout Mode**, **L Spill**, or **R Spill** buttons of the Master Module, the surface is not in Banking mode.

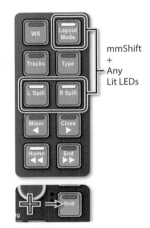

mmShift
+
Any
Lit LEDs

To clear other modes and enter basic Banking mode:

- Press **mmShift** + each lit button among the Navigation buttons.
- Continue until none of these LEDs remain lit.

Navigation buttons

With all these LEDs off, the S6 is in basic Banking mode.

What's In The Bank?

To display overflow tracks to the surface, you need to "bank" or slip the view over, revealing them. Banking is like scrolling your computer screen horizontally to reveal out-of-frame images. Tracks may be banked left or right, one at a time (also called nudging), or eight or more at a time.

The S6's banking paradigm is that the surface is a window displaying the tracks within its view. When you bank right, that *window* moves to the right, showing faders that had been off-screen right, hiding faders that had been on the left. Banking left moves the view to the left, revealing faders that had been hidden on the left, hiding those on the right. The paradigm is the same for all banking functions on the S6.

Easy Banking

The easiest way to bank tracks is to press the modifier keys, **User 1** or **User 2** at the bottom of the fader modules. These keys will bank eight tracks at a time (*see "Modifier Keys" on page 40*).

Banking Buttons

Modifier keys

A set of buttons located among the Navigation buttons on the left side of the lower Master Module give you more detailed control of banking; the Bank and Nudge (**B&N**) buttons.

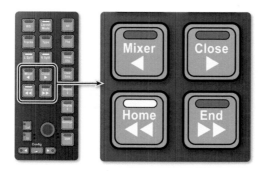

Bank and nudge (B&N) in the Navigation buttons

- Single arrow buttons (◀ ▶) nudge one track at a time. (The labels **Mixer** and **Close** refer to unrelated **mmShift**-modified actions.)
- Double arrow buttons (◀◀ ▶▶) bank eight tracks at a time. Preference settings can change them to bank the entire surface.
- Hold **mmShift** while pressing "◀◀" or "▶▶" and the first or last track of the session will bank to the surface (thus the **Home** and **End** labels).
- When the B&N button LEDs are unlit, there are no tracks available to be banked.
- Colored LEDs lit on any **B&N** button indicate that a Spill Zone is active and those buttons will only affect a spill zone (*see "Using Spill Zones "on page 127*).

Auto-Banking

Activate Auto-Banking and whenever a track is selected, either from the Tracks grid, or from the Pro Tools session, it will be automatically banked to the first channel strip of the surface. This method may work best for users who utilize the Tracks Screen matrix to make track selections.

A setting within Auto-Banking mode limits Auto-Banking to tracks which are not already on the surface when they are selected; if they are already displayed, they will remain in whichever channel strip they sit. Any method of selecting will work while this mode is turned on.

To activate Auto-Banking:

- Navigate to **Settings > User > Surface > Banking**.
- Check **Auto-Bank to Selected Track Mode**.
  - Select **If Not Visible on Surface** or **Always**.

You may love Auto-Banking, but this feature drives me crazy. Selecting the track, which I do frequently when mixing, may jump unwanted tracks to the surface, after which I must struggle to re-bank the surface back the way I had it. If "not visible" is active, it feels erratic; just when I expect a track to leap into my fingers, it does not leap and I must search for it. I discover that is it already on the surface down in strip number 19.

"Scroll to Track" Banking

Another way to move a track into view on the surface is by using the Scroll to Track commands in Pro Tools. Scroll to Track enables you to search by the track name. This, of course, moves your own attention away from the surface and into the Pro Tools window, but it may work for you.

To enable Scroll to Track:

In Pro Tools go to **Preferences... > Mixing > Controllers/"Scroll to Track" Banks Controllers.**

To use Scroll to Track, do one of these in the Pro Tools window:

- Select **Track > Scroll to Track**
- On the keyboard, type **Option + Command + f**
  - Enter the track name, then **OK.**

Locking A Strip

Strips may be locked in place to the surface – immune to banking. Other tracks will bank around locked strips if **Bank Around Locked Strips** is checked in **Settings > User > Surface > Strips**. This can be handy if you want to place your sub-masters and masters (and with them, their meters) into the right-most eight tracks, where they will always remain visible. There is a separate "bank around" setting for Banking Mode and Layout Mode.[3]

---

3. Settings > User > Strips > Bank Around Locked Strips

To lock or unlock a strip:

1. Hold the **Attention** (△) button of the strip that you want to lock.
2. "**Lock**" will appear in the track's OLED.
3. The **Menu** button's LED will light magenta.
4. Continue holding the **Attention** (△) button and press the **Menu** button to toggle the Lock status.

Lock a channel strip

Lock Indicator

Lock Toggle

Channel strip OLED

Locked strips will display a little padlock in the OLED.

Setting Automation Modes with the Channel Strip

While mixing, you must be able to quickly set the automation mode of an individual track, groups of tracks, or all tracks. It is also useful to know to what mode a track is set. The S6 will show you how to do this.

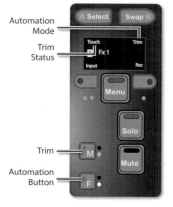

Automation Mode

Trim Status

Trim

Automation Button

Fader strip automation controls

Automation modes may be set using the fader section, the Attention Track fader, the Tracks Screen or the Soft Key pads + **Select** buttons.

Multiple tracks in your session may be set to a desired automation mode by holding the **Do To All** (**Opt** key modifier) or the **Do To Selected** (**Opt** + **Shift** key modifiers).

The current automation mode of a track is indicated in the top-left corner of the trackv OLED.

Using The F Button (Automation Mode Button)

No, I'm not swearing. The simplest way to change the Automation Mode of a track is to press the **F** (Automation Mode) button[4] on the fader section of the track's channel strip. Each press of the **F** button cycles that track to the next automation mode: **off**, **Read**, **Touch**, **Latch**, **Touch/Latch**, then back through the list again.

---

4. Why is "F" used for the button which switches automation modes? That is a mystery.

When the transport is moving, `write` mode is skipped for our safety. `write` can be selected using the Soft Key Pad or Tracks Screen, or when the transport is stopped. *See below.*

The **Opt/Win** and **Shift** modifier keys work just as they do with most Pro Tools actions: **OPT/Win** works as **Do To All** modifier and, **Shift** restricts the action to selected tracks.

To change automation mode of all tracks with the F button:

- Hold down the **Opt/Win** modifier key then press the **F** button. All tracks will cycle through the same automation modes.

To change automation mode of all *selected* tracks with the F button:

- Hold down the **Opt/Win** + **Shift** modifier keys then press the **F** button.

All *selected* tracks will cycle through the same automation modes.

The LEDs next to F indicate its automation writing status:

- No Light=Automation Off   • Green=Read   • Red=Any write mode
- Flashing red when stopped means Latch Prime is activated and primed.
- Flashing red when rolling forward means automation is being written.

F Button Limitations

The F button does not provide a way to directly set a specific automation mode – it instead cycles through them. Making direct changes to the automation mode requires using a Soft Key pad.

Trim Automation Mode can *usually* be toggled on or off by pressing the **M** button on the fader section (*see "Trim Mode Behavior" on page 75*). When Trim is active, the OLED will display "Trim." The LEDs next to **M** are not implemented.

Setting Automation Modes with the Soft Key Pads

We have not yet covered Soft Key pads, but it is coming up soon. Soft Key pads are incredibly helpful when trying to change automation modes, so while we are on that subject, let's cheat a little and take a quick diversion into using Soft Key pads for this one purpose.

Prepare to Set Automation Mode Using a Soft Key Pad

To change automation modes using a Soft Key pad you must get an appropriate Soft Key page assigned to a Soft Key pad.

If **Automation 1** and **Automation 2** are not currently displayed on an available Soft Key pad:

- Press **Shift** (modifier key) **+ 0** (on numeric keypad).

Automation 1 Soft Key page

Preview

The most powerful automation auditioning tool in Pro Tools is available on the Automation 2 Soft Key page. **Preview**, **Punch Preview**, **Suspend Preview**, and **Write To...** commands are there in easy reach.

To set the automation mode of a track (or tracks):

1. Press and hold the Soft Key button of the mode you wish to assign.
2. While holding that button, assign by doing one of these:
   - Press the **F** button of any track which you want set to that automation mode.
   - Press the **Select** button of any track.
   - Touch the track icon in the Tracks Screen track matrix.
   - Touch the track icon in the Track scroller of the home screen.

Automation Mode Soft Keys

Three hands would be required to apply Option or Option + Shift key modifiers to your selection, so there are **Do to All** and **Do to Selected** buttons on the Soft Key pad for this purpose.

Using Do To All or Do To Selected in Soft Key Pad

To assign an automation mode to selected tracks

1. Select the tracks by pressing a **Select** button on a channel strip or pressing ⌘ + the **Select** button on multiple strips, or any other way that you know to select tracks.
2. Press **Do To Selected** in the Soft Key pad.
3. Press the desired automation mode on the Soft Key pad, such as **Touch** or **Latch**.

Automation do to selected

All selected tracks will switch to the chosen mode and the **Do To Selected** button will disengage.

To assign an automation mode to All tracks

1. Press **Do To All** on the Soft Key Pad. The **Do To All** icon will highlight and the Soft Key button will light.
2. Press the desired automation mode and all tracks will switch to that automation mode.

All tracks will switch to the chosen mode and the **Do To Selected** button will disengage.

Automation do to all

Latching Do To All/Selected

Both **Do to All** and **Do to Selected** buttons will latch *on* if double-pressed. When latched, the button LED and the icon will flash. Press once to disengage. Either button may be held down to do multiple actions and will disengage when let go.

Matching Out of Automation

Once you begin adjusting already-written automation you will often want to stop writing without the parameters instantaneously leaping to their underlying positions. You may want them to glide from their writing position to their underlying position. This is called Matching Out.

The amount of time that the system takes to shift to the match position is called the AutoMatch Time, and it is set in Pro Tools. Go to the Pro Tools menu; **Setup > Preferences... > Mixing > Automation/AutoMatch Time** to change the match duration.

When writing in Touch mode, letting go of a control will automatically match it out. When writing in **Write** or **Latch** mode the system must be commanded when to match.

To match out of all automation of a channel:

- Press **F** while writing.

To match out of Volume automation only:

- Of one channel:
  - Press **Command** (Modifier key) **+ F** button.
- Of all channels:
  - Press **Option** (Modifier key) **+ F** button.

To match out of all automation of an individual type (such as Volume or Plug-Ins):

Press **Command** (Modifier key) **+** an Automation Enable Soft Key on Automation 3 Soft key page.

To match out of all automation that is currently writing:

- Press **Auto-Match** Soft Key (Automation Page 2).

The Purpose of the Process Section

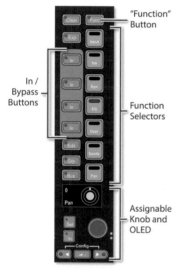

"Function" Button

In / Bypass Buttons

Function Selectors

Assignable Knob and OLED

Process Section controls

The Process Section is where users assign functions such as plug-ins or sends to the Knob Section, where those knobs control the function's parameters. Users may also toggle the bypass status of families of processes within a track, enable editing of clips via the S6 surface, reset parameters to default, and enable automation functions.

Using the Process Section

Pressing one of the Function selector buttons assigns **Input**, **Inserts**, **Dynamics**, **EQ's**, **Sends**, **Pans**, Groups (**Grp**) or Busses (**Bus**) to the Knob Section, lighting that button's LED. The **User** button assigns Instrument plug-ins to the Knob Section.

Multiple Plug-Ins

If the track contains more than one plug-in of the same type, for example if two different EQ's are instantiated, pressing the **EQ** Function select button once will focus the first EQ, pressing twice quickly will focus the second **EQ** and so on. It works the same way for Dynamics, Ins, Sends, etc.

To assign Functions to the Knob Section:

1. Among the Function Selectors, press the desired function type.
   It will be assigned to the Knob Section.
   a. If there are more than one function in the chosen type, the name of those functions will spill into the Knob Section.
   b. If there are more than four functions in the chosen type:
      i. The name of the first four functions will spill into the Knob Section.

    ii. Press the Function selector button quickly and the next four functions will spill into the Knob Section.

2. Press the knob top of the desired function in the Knob Section and the first four parameters of the function will appear on the four knobs.

To assign Inserts to the Knob section:

"Inserts" covers all types of plug-ins, including the EQs and Dynamics plug-ins which are alternately selectable with **EQ** or **DYN** buttons described above.

1. Press **Ins** and the names of the first four inserts (i.e., plug-ins) of a track will spill onto the Knob Section of that channel strip.
   a. If there are more than four inserts in a track, nudge through the inserts using the Navigation buttons below the knobs in the Knob Section.
2. Press the knob top of the desired insert to select it. The first four parameters of that insert will spill into the knobs of the Knob Section of that channel strip.
3. If there are more than four parameters in an insert, after you have selected the insert, you may nudge through the parameters using the Navigation buttons below the knobs.
4. Press the lighted Back (◢▬▬◣) button to navigate up from parameter level to plug-in level if you want to change which plug-in is being controlled.

"Wait a minute!" you may say. "Aren't EQs and dynamics plug-ins also inserts? Why the separate buttons?"

*Avid gave EQ and dynamic plug-ins a special shortcut status on the S6. Using an **EQ** or **Dyn** button only accesses the EQs or Dynamics plug-ins. Using the **Ins** button accesses all instantiated plug-ins (inserts), including EQ and Dynamics.*

*To muddy the waters further, **Edit**, **Grp**, **User**, and **Bus** are not really processes, but they needed to land somewhere, and this is where. This is no problem as long as we do not take the title "Process Section" too seriously.*

Apply Process Section choices to All Tracks.

Normally, actions taken in the Process Section affect only the channel strip in which they are taken. Some mixers find it more effective if they link the process selection of all the tracks so that the same process is called to the Knob section of every track strip.

To assign the same function into the Knob section of every track

- Activate the **All** button in the lower Master Module's navigation section.
  - Any selection will be applied to all tracks.

For example, activate **All**, press **EQ**, and the first four parameters of the first EQ will spill to the Knob section of all tracks which contain an EQ.

The In Buttons

In buttons are a bit of a throwback from earlier mixing consoles which utilized their own proprietary functions, especially EQ and dynamics. **In** would activate that function in that track. When **In** was dark, that function was not active.

Nowadays functions are bit more complicated, since mixers may use any plug-ins available, and sometimes use more than one plug-in of the same type. Mixers commonly write the automation of their plug-ins to neutral setting with the bypass off, then write active settings when needed. Mixers who work like this generally ignore the In buttons.

Using the In Buttons

To best use the **In** buttons, you would write the automation for all functions with bypass set and possibly with some useful or common parameter settings. When needed, you would activate the function with the **In** button, writing the Bypass to Off and adjusting the function as needed.

When **In** is dark, it indicates that all the functions within its scope are bypassed.

Bypassing Functions – Dyn or EQ

Process Section "In" buttons

Pressing the **In** button next to **Dyn** or **EQ** toggles the Bypass button of the currently focused plug-in within its type. For example, press **In** on the **EQ** button and the EQ's bypass will toggle.

If there are more than one plug-in of the type (2 EQ's for example) the last focused plug-in will toggle when **In** is pressed. There is no indication as to which plug-in was last focused, so unless you have recently focused it this can feel rather haphazard if there are more than one plug-in of the type. The LED on the **In** button lights if any plug-in is not bypassed so if multiple plug-ins have the same bypass state, this feature is not very helpful.

Bypassing Functions – Ins (Inserts)

Pressing the **In** button next to **Ins** affects the bypass state of all plug-ins in the channel. If any plug-ins are not already bypassed (LED lit), **In** will bypass them all. If all plug-ins in the channel are bypassed (LED not lit), In will un-bypass them.

I am not convinced that the In buttons are helpful. Save these for later in your S6 training and see if they bring you happiness then.

The Grp Button

When **Grp** is pressed, the first four of the session's track groups (if any exist) are displayed on knobs of the Knob Section. Additional groups, if present, may be nudged to the section using the Navigation buttons at the bottom of that Knob section. If Knob Expand[5] is active, the first 32 track groups are displayed in the Knob Module.

The **In** button LED of a group's knob cluster will light if that track is a member of that group.

The track's membership in a group can be toggled by pressing the button top in the Knob Section, or the **In** button in the Knob Section.

To use the Group button:

1. Press **Grp** button.
   The **In** button will light if the track is a group member.
2. Press the **In** button to add or remove the track from that group.

The Func Button

This button is scary-powerful. It enables automation for any un-enabled parameters in the focused EQ, Dynamics or Insert function (plug-in). It gives no warning, and unless you are watching the plug-in's window very closely when it happens, you may not know it happened. I suggest you never ever touch it.

---

5. Knob Expand is indicated by a lit **Exp** button. See "Expand Knobs Mode" on page 93.

I am not a fan of instantiating plug-ins from the S6 surface, but maybe that is because I have been using Pro Tools so long that it takes me no time at all to do this in the Pro Tools window. I am also not a fan of dynamically enabling automation during a mix because it can cause global changes to that mix. I recommend that you enable and anchor automation for every parameter of every function in every track before you begin. If you do that, this button will pose no threat.

The **Clear** Button allows users to reset a channel strip, a function, or a parameter to its default state. It does nothing to the underlying automation; it simply sets the parameter to default at that moment, same as touching a control while holding down the **Opt/Win** modifier key. This could be very useful when creating templates wherein you wish all settings to be at their default.

Top of the Process
Section

To reset to default (clear):

1. Press **Clear** to activate reset (clear) mode.
   The **Clear** Button's LED will flash red and controls which can be reset will light.
2. While Clear is flashing do one of these:
   - To clear a fader to unity, press **F** on the Fader Module or touch the fader itself.
   - To reset one parameter, touch or press its lit control. If the parameter is showing on a knob of the knob module, press the knob.
   - To reset all parameters of a function, press the desired function button in the Process Section (such as **EQ**, **Dyn**, or **Pan**). Not all functions support **Clear**.
   - To reset all parameters of the channel strip, press the **Select** button on the fader section.

After clearing, the **Clear** Button will de-activate. To de-activate it without clearing anything, press **Clear** while it is flashing.

The Assignable Knob

At the bottom of each Process Section is an Assignable Knob. By default this knob controls the front panner of its track. It can be assigned to control any parameter, but most users leave it as an "always-there" pan control (*see "Assigning an Assignable Knob" on page 198 if you want to exercise your individuality*).

Using the Assignable Knob in Place of the Knob Section

Some installations of the S6 do not include a Knob Section, which is a shame. This Assignable Knob can be used to adjust settings of plug-ins. It is slower going than the Knob Module, but better than nothing. Most mixers will use the Workstation screen instead.

To use the Assignable Knob to adjust plug-in settings:

1. Press **Back** (◢▬▬◣) + **Ins** on the Process Section.
   - The name of the first plug-in of the track will display in the OLED.
2. If there are more than one plug-in in the track, press ▶ or ◀ to display the next or previous.
3. When the desired plug-in is displayed, press the knob.
   - The **Back** LED will light, indicating that a plug-in is selected.
   - Use the knob to adjust the setting.
   - Use ▶ or ◀ to navigate through the plug-in's parameters.
4. Press **Back** to exit the plug-in.

Using the Knob Section

For the next page or two, things get messy. There are only four knobs available in the Knob section for each track, and accessing parameters of plug-ins which have many parameters requires banking within the Knob Section, which takes a kind of internal focus and patience that I do not always possess. Do not fret too much because there is a cleaner way to deal with functions; Strip Expand Mode. That will be explored in a later section.

Bringing a Parameter to the Surface in the Knob Section

The Knob Section is the place where your functions meet your surface. Once functions are sent here you can tweak, twist, and adjust them. But just because a function has been assigned to the Knob Section does not mean that the parameter you want is available – yet. If the parameter you want does not pop up as the default, you will need to nudge to it. There is a clear hierarchy of how those functions and parameters are accessed in the Knob Section.

Navigate to the desired function parameter in the Knob Section:

1. Press a Function Selector button *(see page 44)* on the Process Section. This sends that function family to the knob module.
   a. If there is only one function of the selected type, go to step 2.
      If there are more than one function of the same type in this track, each individual function's name will be assigned to a knob.
      If there are five or more functions in the function family:
      Nudge to the desired function using the Navigation buttons at the bottom of the Knob section.
   b. Press the knob top of the desired function to select it.
2. Is the desired parameter showing on the knobs?
   a. If yes, smile and go to step 3, otherwise…
   b. Nudge to the desired parameter using the Navigation buttons at the bottom of the Knob section.
3. Congratulations! You have found your parameter. Make your adjustment and move on.

For example, if you press the **DYN** button on the Process Section of a track which has a compressor plug-in, the four knobs of that tracks' Knob section will be assigned to the first four parameters of the compressor: **Threshold**, **Ratio**, **Attack**, and **Release**. To access additional parameters of the function, use the Knob Section Navigation buttons.

If there are more than one dynamic function their names appear on the knobs. Pressing on the knob top moves down one level to display parameter banks.

When there are more than four dynamic functions, banking may be required to find the desired function. Use the Navigation buttons at the bottom of the Knob section.

Using the Knob Section Navigation Buttons

At the bottom of each column of the Knob Section is a set of buttons which nudge groups of parameters of the assigned function to the knobs, four parameters at a time.

- The " ◀ " and " ▶ " buttons at the bottom of the Knob section nudge groups of four parameters. They light when this is possible.
- The Back (◢━━━┙) button, between the " ◀ " and " ▶ ," navigates up one level. It will light when that is possible.

Knob Section
Navigation buttons

The word "**Config**" printed above every **Back** button refers to a simultaneous press of both " ◀ " and " ▶ ." This action is not implemented at this time on the S6. *I think Avid should supply black stickers to cover over the unnecessary "Config" labels, but they probably will not do so.*

Knob Cluster Behavior

In the Knob Section, each track has four knob "clusters." Each cluster contains a velocity-sensitive[6] knob, an OLED, a **Sel** and **In** button. Each active knob cluster will take on the parameters of the assigned control.

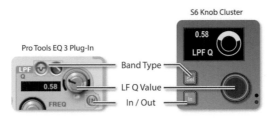

Knob Cluster controls

Look at the Low Frequency Q control of the Pro Tools EQ3.

This plug-in control has:
- A knob which adjusts the Q value.
- An In/Out switch to bypass the filter.
- A Band Type switch selects the band type.

The Knob Cluster assignment:
- The knob adjusts the EQ3's LFQ setting.
- The **In** button toggles the LFQ's In/Out switch.
- The **Sel** button changes the Band Type.

If there is no **In/Out** switch on an assigned control, the **In** button is inactive.

On some controls the **Sel** button may assign the knob to a secondary parameter.

For example, **Sel** will switch the knob assignment between Q and Frequency on many EQ's. It will switch between Pre- and Post-fader on a send. It may behave differently than you expect.

---

6. The faster you twist a velocity-sensitive knob, the further it goes with one twist. Slow movement is supposed to give finer adjustments. Speed and sensitivity can be adjusted in Settings > User > Knobs.

> I do not know about you, but I find this whole thing confusing and complicated.
>
> Using the four knobs of the Knob Section in a channel strip is best suited to controlling simpler functions with four or fewer parameters. such as a basic compressor, a send, or a stereo panner. Banking around to find parameters never makes you look good to the client.
>
> The inconsistency of the **Sel** buttons is confusing unless you study and memorize the behavior of specific plug-ins.
>
> The good news is that the S6 features a much better way to operate complex functions: Strip Expand Mode. It is explained in "Expand Knobs Mode" on page 113.

Using the Display Section

The Avid S6 is designed to allow the mixer to turn away from the Pro Tools screen and mix exclusively with the surface controls. The Display Section is the window into the source material as well as many functions and processes within the tracks.

Each display module provides a virtual display section for each of the eight channel strips of its chassis section.

The S6 provides seven different display options, called Display Layouts.

Different layouts show different combinations of these features:

- Input Meters (large or small). There is an input meter on every Display Layout
- Waveforms (the zoom scale setting may be changed)
- Functions (Pans, Inserts, EQ plug-ins, Dynamics Plug-ins)
- Function graphs (for selected function types)
- Input/Output Routing
- Automation mode

Feature	1. Large Meters	2. Large Waveforms	3. Meters and Waveforms	4. Meters and Function	5. Waveforms and Function	6. Waveform and Dual Functions	7. Waveforms and Dual Functions + Routes
Standard Features	X	X	X	X	X	X	X
I/O Assignment	X	X		X	X		X

Feature	1. Large Meters	2. Large Waveforms	3. Meters and Waveforms	4. Meters and Function	5. Waveforms and Function	6. Wave- form and Dual Functions	7. Waveforms and Dual Functions + Routes
Automation Mode	X	X		X	X		X
Large Meter (Multi)	X						
Medium Meter		X					
Medium Narrow Meter (Mono)					X	X	
Small Meter (Multi)			X				X
Short Wide Waveform			X				
Medium Narrow Waveform					X	X	
Short Narrow Waveform							X
Function Display				1	1	2	2
Function Display or Knob Module Assignments				X	X	X	X

By default, all channel strips will show the same Display Layout, but individual channel strips may be set to show different layouts.

All Display Layouts have these features:

- The name, and color of the track at the bottom of the meter.
- Gain reduction meter (to the right of main meter).
- Optionally, track number and workstation number (modifiable in User Settings).
- Muted tracks will be dimmed.
- Soloed tracks are displayed normal, while non-soloed tracks are dimmed.
- Meters which follow the scale and ballistics of Pro Tools system.
- Most layouts show the name and page number of the function which is currently assigned to the Knob Section.

All Display Layouts with waveforms have these features:

- The name of the incoming clip displayed above the waveform area.
- The name of the outgoing clip displayed below the waveform area.
- Adjustable waveform zoom scale and opacity.
- When a track displays automation data in the Pro Tools window:
  - Automation data can optionally be overlaid on the waveform.
  - The direction of + and − on the automation data can be reversed left-right.

Display Layout descriptions (see illustration below):

1. Large Meters
- Large multi-channel meter
- I/O Assignments
- Automation Mode indicator

2. Large Waveforms
- Large meter (mono)
- Long narrow waveform (mono or stereo only)
  - (surround formats show single summed waveform)
- I/O Assignments
- Automation Mode indicator

3. Meters and Waveforms
- Small meter (multi-channel)
- Short wide waveform
- No I/O assignments

4. Meters and Function (system default display mode)
- Medium meter
- 1 Function display –
  - If EQ, Dynamics Plug-In or Pan is selected in the channel strip, a function graph is displayed
  - If the above functions are not selected, the current Knob Module knob assignment displayed
- A bouncing ball representing gain reduction is shown on Dynamics plug-ins which support the feature
- I/O Assignments
- Automation Mode indicator

5. Waveforms and Function
- Medium, narrow meter (mono)
- Short narrow waveform (mono or stereo only)
  - (Surround formats show single summed waveform)
- 1 Function display –
  - If EQ, Dynamics Plug-In or Pan is selected in the channel strip, a function graph is displayed.
  - If above functions are not selected, the name of the current Knob Module knob assignment is displayed.
- Dynamics plug-ins that support it show a bouncing ball representing gain reduction
- I/O Assignments
- Automation Mode indicator

6. Waveforms and Dual Functions

- Medium, narrow meter (mono)
- Medium, narrow waveform
- 2 Function displays –
  - ○ If EQ, Dynamics Plug-In or Pan is selected in the channel strip, its function graph is displayed.
  - ○ If above functions are not selected, the name of the current Knob Module knob assignment displayed.
- Dynamics plug-ins that support it show a bouncing ball representing gain reduction.
- No I/O shown.

7. Waveforms and Dual Functions + Route

- Same as Waveforms and Dual Functions, but add:
  - ○ I/O Assignments
  - ○ Automation Mode indicator

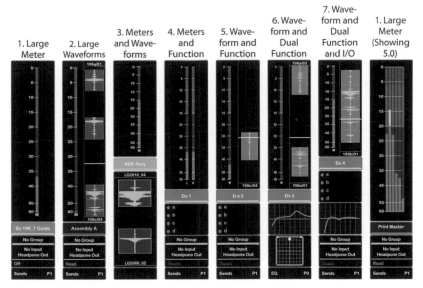

The seven standard Display Layouts

Changing the Display Layout

The Display Layout may be changed persistently in the S6's User Preferences, or temporarily using surface buttons.

Changing the Display Layout From the Surface

Layout preferences may be saved to User Preferences, but they are quite easy to change as you work by using buttons on the Master Module.

To change the Display Layout of all strips:

- Press **mmShift + Display 1** or **mmShift + Display 2** to cycle through the seven Display Layouts,

To change the Display Layout of an individual strip (only accomplished on the surface):

1. Press and hold the Attention (△) button.
The **Select** button LED will light, and the word Meter will display on the top-left corner of that track's fader OLED.
2. Press the **Select** button to cycle that strip's meter through the seven Display Layouts.

To revert a channel back to the same view as the rest of the tracks:

- On the Channel Strip of the track you want to revert, hold `Select` for 2 seconds.

To change the Display Layout preference:

1. On the Touchscreen, navigate to **Settings > User > Display Module > Display**.
2. Select the desired Display Layout from the pull-down.
3. Save the User Preferences file or the Pro Tools session if so configured.

Waveform Display

One of several cool features of the Display Section is that it can depict (when set to a waveform Display Layout) the audio in a track as if it is moving past the play-head. This is comparable to the timeline of Pro Tools, but the audio waveforms move from top to bottom when playing forward. A marker indicates the playhead position.

To show waveform on the display module:

- Select a Display Layout which includes a Waveform Display (Display 2, 3, 5, 6, or 7)

Waveform Scale (Zoom)

On layouts which show a waveform display, the scale of the waveform may be adjusted, showing a longer or shorter time. The amplitude of the waveform does not change, only the time scale. To change the zoom scale of the waveform displays of a strip:

- Press **Display 1** to zoom in.
- Press **Display 2** to zoom out.

The zoom scale will change in ten-second increments.

Showing Automation on Track Display:

One of the most helpful features of the Display Section is available on Display Layouts which show a waveform. You may overlay an image of one lane of automation data on the waveform, typically volume automation. This display mimics the volume automation display in Pro Tools. When automation is being written, the parameter line turns red, showing the difference between values being written, and those already written. This can be very helpful when attempting to match out of an automation writing pass.

Automation data display is most helpful when the waveform zoom setting is close enough to distinguish automation breakpoints. (*See "Waveform zoom" on page 153 for zoom setting information.*)

The opacity of the data overlay can be adjusted, and the left/right orientation can be inverted.

For an automation lane to be shown in the S6 display, it must currently be showing on the Pro Tools track.

To configure and enable automation data overlay in the Settings:

1. On the Touchscreen, navigate to **Settings > User > Display Module > Common**.
2. Configure the following settings as desired:
   - **Show Automation** – enables automation display.
   - **Reverse Automation Lanes** – inverts left/right orientation of the automation display.
   - **Automation Opacity** – set from 0% to 100%. At 0% a thin line is shown.
3. In **Display Module > Display** touch the **Layout** pull-down and choose a view which displays waveforms:
   - **2. Large Waveforms**
   - **3. Meters and Waveforms**
   - **5. Waveforms and Function**
   - **6. Waveforms and Dual Functions**
   - **7. Waveforms and Dual Functions + Route**

4. Set the displayed tracks to show the desired automation lane by doing one of these:

- Hold **Shift + Option + Command** and touch any control on the surface. (i.e. touch a Fader to show volume).
- In Pro Tools use the Track View Selector to show the desired automation lane.

Once this mode is set, you can toggle it for individual tracks, all tracks or selected tracks.

Pro Tools: Track View selector

To enable data overlay:

- For one track:
  - ○ Press **Ctrl + ⌘/Alt** (modifier keys) + touch desired parameter's control.
- For selected tracks:
  - ○ Press **Ctrl + ⌘/Alt + Shift** (modifier keys) + touch desired parameter's control.
- For all tracks:
  - ○ Press **Ctrl + ⌘/Alt + Shift + Opt/Win** (modifier keys) + touch desired parameter's control.

To disable data overlay:

- For one track:
  - ○ Press **Ctrl + ⌘/Alt** (modifier keys) **+ Select** on the channel strip.
- For selected tracks:
  - ○ Press **Ctrl + ⌘/Alt + Shift** (modifier keys) **+ Select** on the channel strip.
- For all tracks:
  - ○ Press **Ctrl + ⌘/Alt + Shift + Opt/Win** (modifier keys) **+ Select** on the channel strip.

Display Feature When Recording Audio:

Recording Indicator

If a track is set to a Display Layout which includes waveforms:

- When the track is Record-Ready, it will flash red, and the track will be outlined in red.
- When the track is actively recording audio, the waveform will show red and will begin writing waveforms of the recorded audio.

Waveform during recording

Bonus Techniques
Trim Mode Behavior

When writing trim automation in **Write** or **Latch** mode, the **M** button *will not* exit Trim mode. This mimics the behavior of Pro Tools.

To exit Trim mode while writing automation in Write or Latch, do one of these:

- Stop playback.
- Change automation mode to Touch, Touch/Latch, Read or Off.
- Match out of Latch or Write by pressing the **F** button, then **M** button.

Trim mode cannot be toggled on while writing automation in Write mode. That is a Pro Tools thing.

Chapter 7

Meters!

Meter Needs

The S6 does not have significant metering built into the basic hardware. On system configurations which sport Display Modules, track meters are available, and these track meters can be set up to display stem and master output levels. Additional Display Modules called Master Display Modules may be installed in the console chassis, and up to two "normal" Display Modules can be commandeered from the existing surface to act as Master Meter Modules. Alternatively, mixers can use any number of great meter plug-ins on the Pro Tools screen, or outputs can be routed through hardware sends to outboard meters of all kinds. We will explore some options available for systems with Display Modules, but be aware that there are other options.

When mixing you need a set of meters which reflect the format and output of the mix. The levels showing on those meters should be the levels which get recorded. Pro Tools allows the user to set all track meters except Master meters to either pre-fader or post-fader.[1] The preferred (and default) setting is pre-fader, which is the most commonly used setting. In this setting mode most meters measure the audio level of the incoming source to that track – before it gets to the fader or other processors. Only the Master meters or meters in a Master Meter Module (*coming up later under "Master Meter Modules" on page 151*) will show post-fader levels. Therefore, the meters showing on most source tracks should not be used to determine levels, since they only show the pre-fader level of audio. Master tracks should be used for output metering.

In cinema mixing, there is commonly a separate meter for each section or stem. There should be one meter each for dialog, music, and effects, and sometimes sub-stems such as SFX, Foley, and BG's. In addition to the stem meters, a composite meter displaying the Print Master is essential. You can accomplish all of this by creating appropriate recording paths and mastering tracks in your workstation sessions.

---

1. Change metering in Pro Tools menu: Options / Pre-Fader Metering.

DOI: 10.4324/9781003111801-9

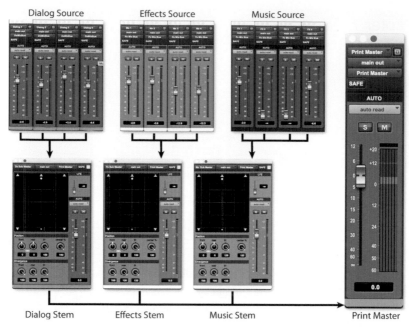

Caption: Stems and Masters

Set the Standard (Of Your Meters)

Whichever method you choose for meter display, you should be sure to set the scale and ballistics of those meters.

1. In Pro Tools go to `Setup > Preferences > Metering > Track and Master Meter Types.`
2. Select the desired meter type.
3. In the `Advanced Meter Type Settings` section, adjust settings to your desired standards.

The track meter scales can be set differently from the Master Meter scales. These Pro Tools settings will apply to all meters in Pro Tools and on the S6.

If you decide to use outboard plug-in meters, read up on those plug-ins and be sure to set them to your desired standards.

Meter Strategies

Quick and Dirty Meters

One "sort-of quick" way to have meters available to you is to scroll the recorder track meters into view on the Touchscreen's Home page Meter Scroller *(see "Additional controls on the Home Screen" on page 103).* If you are not using recorder tracks in your project, be sure that you have a sub-master fader for each stem and the Print Master. Scroll them into view on the Meter Scroller. Do not touch them. They are not very big, but they are there.

Meter Scroller has very small meters

Spill Zone Meters

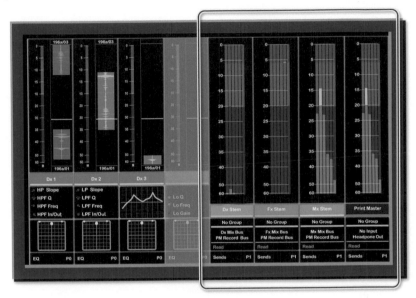

Spill Zone meters

If your mixing style allows you to allocate surface channels in a spill zone to sub-masters and master(s) you can lock a group of meters which represent the outputs of those channels. If you are not yet comfortable with creating Track Layouts or creating Spill Zones, you may need to skip ahead to "Creating Track Layouts" on page 140 and "Configuring Spill Zones" on page 126.

To create spill zone meters:

1. Create a Track Layout which includes the submasters and master track(s).
   - Make the layout only as wide as necessary.
   - I suggest that you place the master on a far side.
     a. Set the Display Layout of each track to something big, like Large Meters.
        i. Press Attention (△) **+ Select** on each channel strip to cycle through layouts.

2. Name, store and save this Track Layout.
3. Configure the desired Spill Zone (*see "Configuring Spill Zones" on page 126*).
   a. Only as wide as needed to hold the above tracks.
   b. Place it at the far end of one side of the surface.
4. Spill the meter Layout into the chosen spill zone. On the Master Module:
   a. Press **Layout Mode**.
   b. Press **R Spill** or **L Spill**.
5. On the Soft Key pad press the button next to the name you gave the meter layout. It will spill into the selected Spill Zone.
6. Lock the submasters and master into their strips:
   a. On each strip, hold **Attention** (△) and press the **Select** button. A padlock icon will appear in the OLED of the strip.
7. In Pro Tools, select the desired metering type (*see "Set the Standard" on page 78*).

Those meter tracks will not be available for mixing, but you *will* have dedicated stem and printmaster meters.

More Complicated, More Better Metering

A more controlled and fruitful method is to create the recorder or master output paths discussed above and instantiate metering plug-ins, such as Insight, LM-2/6 or K-Meter, into those tracks. Make the plug-in window(s) persistent by turning off the target indicator in the top-right corner.

These plug-ins must be displayed somewhere, either on the picture monitor or on the DAW monitor, taking up some screen real estate. Be sure to set each meter to the same scale.

Target indicator of a plug-in

Metering That's Too Cool (Complicated) for School

The S6 allows users to re-configure the surface designating one of the Display Modules to be a Master Meter Module. The tracks that are to be displayed in the Master Meter Module must be defined in "Meter Layouts." You gain a dedicated meter display, but you lose the display for any tracks in that chassis section of the console. This is an advanced process, and you must change the configuration of the console for it to work. It is a great way to achieve industry-standard metering, but it changes the surface configuration, which is not allowed in some situations.

In many settings, changing the surface configuration could make the console confusing or unusable to others, and it could invoke the rancor of the engineers of your mix room or school, so do not do it without getting express permission from the proper authorities.

Be kind to your colleagues and put the configuration back to the studio standard before you wrap for the day (or night). When you are ready to try it, see "Master Meter Modules" on page 151.

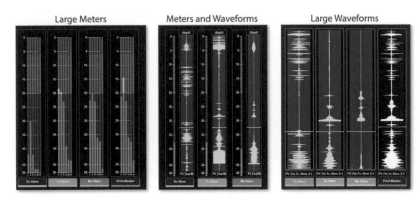

Master Meter types

Fader Meters – What's All That Flashing About?

Back in Chapter 1 we mentioned the little LED meters which are embedded in the fader section just to the left of each fader. Other than the input meter, these are not level meters, only displays of specific elements of the automation, but they look like meters to Avid and to me.

Input Meter

Two LED strips to the left of each fader are audio input meters. They usually show the incoming (pre-fader) level of the audio that is playing in the track. The displayed level is not affected by the fader setting. It only shows that there is source audio playing in this track. If the source track is monaural, only the left column of LEDs will light. If it is stereo or wider, both outer columns will light. This is (more or less) the same information which is showing on the Display Module at the top end of the channel strip.

Go to **Options** and de-select **Pre-Fader Metering**. This setting changes all meters in Pro Tools and the S6 except for Master faders, which always show post-fader levels.

Input meter

Most mixers I know prefer to keep all source tracks set to pre-fader metering. This gives them a visual clue about which tracks have content as the session plays, regardless of their fader setting. That little jiggle of pulsing light sometimes helps them find their way in a large or complex session.

Gain Reduction Meter

Nestled between the two audio meter strips is a smaller center meter strip which indicates the amount of gain reduction being applied by a compressor or other plug-in instantiated in that track.

The gain reduction indicator starts at the top – the more gain reduction, the more the LEDs flash downward – the opposite direction of the input meters. If you see it doing a lot of downward movement, beware; you may be over-compressing. This data, too, is shown on the Display Module at the top end of the channel strip.

Gain reduction

Underlying Automation Meter

When writing direct volume automation (not in Trim mode), the right meter shows the underlying automation level. Those three LEDs slide up and down the length of the fader path, and if you stop writing automation when the fader is lined up to them, you will have pretty good level match.

This feature is a little tricky to use, but with some practice, you may find it a good helper.

Underlying automation

Trim Meter

When writing an initial Trim pass, the right meter will display at "0" to indicate that Trim automation is being written.

When writing Trim automation after the initial pass, LEDs show the un-coalesced trim value above or below 0 dB. This is the same as the yellow line you might see in Pro Tools when displaying volume automation while trim automation is un-coalesced. If that value is below 0 dB, the LEDs will light beginning at 0 and extending downward to the current values. If it is above 0, the LEDs will light beginning at 0 and extending upward. If you are trying to match that value with your trim fader, you must chase either the top of the LED column (above 0 trim value) or the bottom of the LED column (below 0 trim value).

Trim automation

Note that this only works when **Coalesce Trim Automation** is set to **On Exiting Trim Mode** or **Manually**, since the other option, **After Every Pass** makes every pass an initial pass.

If the underlying automation data is moving very much, it is hard to catch it using these last two indicators. I find it better to display this data on the Display module and watch that instead.

Chapter 8

Three Ways to Approach Mixing

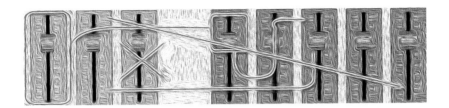

Here we will explore three great ways to approach mixing:

- VCA masters
- Attentioned tracks
- Strip Expand modes

These are not the only three ways, and they are not exclusive to one-another. They play well together. Most mixers intermingle them as needed. Using VCA Masters may also involve Spill Zones, which will be covered soon (*see "Using Spill Zones" on page* 127 *for more detail*).

VCA's and How They Started

Within Pro Tools, tracks can be assigned to one or more groups. The volume level of all members of a group can be controlled by a single track called a VCA Master track (*see below*), making it easy to make relative level changes across the group members using one fader. Mixers sometimes find that individual members of the group (GMs)[1] need to be adjusted rather than the entire group. One way to do that is to scroll through the tracks and find the individual tracks to adjust. Another way is to have the system "spill" the GMs of a selected VCA Master onto the surface where they can be found and adjusted more easily. Those GM tracks are "spilled" onto the surface somewhere. One great place to which they may be spilled is into Spill Zones. There are other easy options as well.

The term VCA refers to a Voltage Controlled Amplifier. VCA's were created in King Arthur's time as a way to give a single fader control over the level of multiple audio channels. An amplifier was placed in the audio chain, post fader, and possibly also

---

1. GM = Group Member.

DOI: 10.4324/9781003111801-10

post-processing. The audio of any GM paths was fed into this amplifier, which was controlled by a fader or knob which they called the VCA Master.

Hundreds of years later, Pro Tools grabbed this idea and created similar capabilities for Pro Tools. Collections of tracks can be grouped together, with all GM volumes controlled by a single VCA Master fader. The volume setting of the VCA Master acts similarly to Trim mode. When the Master sits at unity, the GMs continue to play their volume automation as written. If the Master is raised or lowered, the GM automation is offset by that amount. If a GM is already playing at +10, the Master cannot cause it to play any louder than +12, only 2 dB above its setting. Any GMs which entered the group with settings of 0 dB or below can only be raised 12 dB with the Master (*see "VCA Masters vs Aux Tracks vs Grouped Tracks" on page 2 for more information*).

Are you Amazed? I Didn't Think So

As fascinating as that is, the more interesting feature of VCA Masters and GMs is one which Pro Tools added to the VCA feature; the ability to spill the GMs of a VCA Master. This gives the mixer some easy tricks to organize tracks during a mix.

Spilling VCA Masters

Avid applies the term "spill" to VCA's as well as Spill Zones. "Spilling" is the assignment of tracks into a spill zone, and it also is used to describe the feature which calls up the members of a VCA Master group and displays them into nearby channel strips. On other mix surfaces this may be called filleting or splaying. Spilling into a spill zone and spilling VCA masters are similar but different functions. The doubled terms can cause some confusion as you learn to use the mighty S6. This is made even more confusing when you want to spill the contents of VCA Masters into Spill Zones; get ready for that later.

Using VCA Master Spilling

Before any VCA Master spilling takes place, you must create the VCA Masters and track groups. If you do not know how to do that, see the current Pro Tools Reference Guide; Chapter 48 – VCA Master Tracks.

Place a VCA Master into a channel strip on the S6 by banking, moving tracks within the workstation, or by creating track layouts. (*see "Track Layouts and the Tracks Screen" on page 133*).

Once a VCA Master is showing on the surface, there are three easy ways to spill its GMs to the surface.

To spill GMs to adjacent strips:

1. Press and hold **Menu** in the VCA Master's channel strip.
2. Press the button to the left or right of **Menu**.

The GMs will spill to that side of the VCA Master, wherever it may be on the surface.

This button push is easily accomplished by pushing the **Menu** button with one finger then rocking to the desired side.

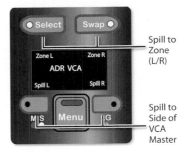

Group member spill controls

To spill GMs to a Spill Zone[2] using the Menu button:

1. Press and hold **Menu** in the VCA Master's channel strip.
   The words **Zone L** and **Zone R** will display in the OLED below the **Select** and **Swap** buttons.
2. Press **Select** to spill to the left spill zone, or **Swap** to spill to the Right Spill zone.

Automatic VCA Spilling

The S6 can be configured to automatically spill VCA members to a spill zone when the VCA Master is attentioned.

To automatically spill GMs to a spill zone – VCA Master to the Attention fader:

1. On the Touchscreen, navigate to **Settings > User > Surface > Attention/ Automatic Spill of Attentioned VCA.**
2. Select the target area for automatic spilling.
   * When assigned to the left or right of the Attention Track Fader the GMs spill to the tracks adjacent to the Master Module section, left or right.
3. Press the Attention button (△) in the VCA Master's fader section to attention and spill.

When spilled, the LED on **Menu** of a VCA Master will show dark green. If spilled to a spill zone, the corresponding **L Spill** or **R Spill** LEDs will also show dark green.

Spill Zone controls

---

2. Spill zones must already be configured. See "Configuring Spill Zones" on page 126.

The **Menu** button LED on spilled GMs will show light green if that option is checked in **Settings** >**User** > **Surface** > **Strips/Spill Zone Menu Key Mode for Layouts, Workstations or Types.**

Banking within Spill Zones

1. If the desired **Spill** button is not white (bright blue), press it.
2. Use the Bank (◀◀ ▶▶) or Nudge (◀ ▶) buttons on the Master Module.

To unspill VCA GMs, do one of the these:

- Press **Menu** on the spilled VCA Master.
- Press **Menu** on one of the spilled GMs.
- Press **mmShift** + **L Spill** or **mmShift** + **R Spill** on the Master Module.
- If using nested VCA Masters.
  - Press **Menu** once to unspill up one layer.
  - Hold **Menu** for more than a second to unspill all VCA layers.

Expanding VCA GMs to Knobs

Wouldn't it be great if you could touch a VCA Master and have its GM's volume controls spill into the Knob Section? And what if you could expand those GMs to use all 32 knobs of the Knob Module? That way you could adjust the individual volume of any individual GM (up to 32 at a time) without disrupting the rest of the console layout. Try one of these methods.

To spill VCA GMs to the Knob Section (4 at a time):

1. Bank the VCA Master strip to the surface.
2. On the Process Module, toggle **Bus** to on.
   The first 4 VCA GMs will populate the Knob Section.
3. If needed, navigate to the desired GMs using the Knob Section's nudge buttons.

To expand VCA GMs to the Knob Module (32 at a time):

1. Bank the VCA Master strip to the surface.
2. On the Process Module, toggle **Bus** to on.
   The first 4 VCA GMs will populate the Knob Section.
3. Press **Exp** on the strip and the GMs will populate the entire Knob Module.

When GMs are assigned to the Knob Section, the **Sel** button toggles **Solo** and the In-button toggles **Mute** for each GM.

To unspill GMs:
• Press the **Menu** button of the VCA Master's strip or on any GM.

Sending VCA GMs to Attention Track Knobs
Just when you thought that was the end of VCA Masters, there is still another way that you can tweak individual GMs; using the Attention Track Knobs, those eight lonely knobs surrounding the Touchscreen.

To spill VCA GMs to the Attention Track Knobs:
1. Bank the VCA Master strip to the surface.
2. On the Touchscreen, navigate to the **Home** page.
3. Press **Attention** (△) button on VCA Master's strip.
4. Touch **Bus** in the Function Scroller.

Bank different VCA GMs to the Attention Track Knobs the same way as any other parameters (*see "Attention Track Knobs" on page 98*).

VCA Master Mixing: What Is It Good For?
What is the value of this VCA Master/GM spilling stuff? Here is an example of how it works for you.

If you create a footsteps VCA Master which controls all the foley footstep tracks (GMs) of the session, you can raise or lower all footstep tracks with that one VCA Master fader, which isn't much more special than using an Aux Sub or by grouping tracks in Pro Tools. Two things *are* special. With a touch of a button on the VCA Master fader channel strip you can easily splay those footstep GM tracks to the surface from wherever they may be in your session, never having to search for them. Once the GMs are exposed, they may be adjusted individually without affecting other members of the VCA group.

Pressing one button will unspill all GMs, jumping back to the previous track layout.

That is nice enough, but it gets better because Pro Tools allows you to put VCA Masters into groups and control them with a more masterly master (aka Nested Masters). You can create layers of nested VCA Masters, each controlling (and being able to spill) other VCA Masters, which in turn may control either lower-level VCA Masters, or individual tracks.

The ability to raise or lower huge swaths of tracks is far less important (or useful) than the ability to easily drill down, layer by layer, to expose individual tracks to the surface for mix adjustments.

Looking at this from the top down, you could create one VCA Master called "Foley" which controls (and spills) two VCA Masters called "Props" and "Footsteps," each of which controls (and spills) the individual Props or Footsteps tracks.

To lower the hero's footsteps, you spill the "Foley" VCA Master, revealing "Props" and "Footsteps," then spill "Footsteps" to reveal all footsteps tracks, then find and lower his footsteps.

Take the idea one step further, and you could hone your entire mix into three nested VCA Masters: Dx, Fx, and Mx, sitting on the surface in front of you.

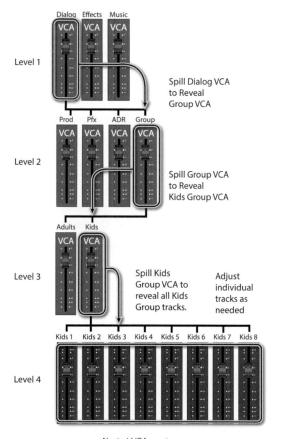

Nested VCA masters

From each of those VCA Masters, you could, without much fuss, drill down through the organization of your mix to find the track or tracks which you might need to adjust.

Need to change the level of a line of Kids Group ADR?

1. From the Dx, Fx, and Mx VCA's (Level 1)

2. Spill Dx VCA to Prod Dx, Pfx, Principal ADR, and Group. (Level 2)

3. Spill the Group ADR VCA to Adult Group and Kids Group. (Level 3)

4. Spill the Kids Group VCA and there are all the Kids Group tracks. (Level 4)

You will not need to scroll or bank or search very hard to reveal the Kids Group tracks onto the surface.

Hold the **Menu** button of one of the spilled VCA GMs for a second, and everything un-spills, leaving Dx, Fx, and Mx VCA Masters alone on the surface in front of you.

Table 8.1 How VCA Master Levels may be designed.

Level 1	Level 2	Level 3	Level 4	Level 5
Dia VCA	Dx VCA	Dx		
	Pfx VCA	Pfx Tracks		
	ADR VCA	Principal ADR Tracks		
	Group VCA	Adult VCA	Adult Tracks	
		Kids VCA	Kids Tracks	
Fx VCA	Foley VCA	Footsteps VCA	Principal FS VCA	Principal FS Tracks
			Crowd FS VCA	Crowd FS
		Props VCA	Props Tracks	
	Autos VCA	Motors VCA	Motor Tracks	
		Tires VCA	Tires Tracks	
		Passby VCA	Passby Tracks	
	Other Fx	Other Fx Subgroup1	Fx Subgrp 1 Tracks	
		Other Fx Subgroup2	Fx Subgrp 2 Tracks	
		Other Fx Subgroup3	Fx Subgrp 3 Tracks	
Mx VCA	Score VCA	LSO VCA	Perc VCA	Perc Tracks
			Brass VCA	Brass Tracks
			Other VCA	Other tracks
		Jazz VCA	Drum VCA	Drum Tracks
			Piano VCA	Piano Tracks
			Bass VCA	Bass Tracks
	Songs VCA	Source VCA	Various sections	
		Songs VCA	Various sections	

Tips on Organizing for VCA masters

If you are going to use VCA Masters in your mix, a bit of pre-planning will make it work more gracefully.

First – you must create the hierarchy of Master and GM groups and VCA's in your Pro Tools session. Some tips:

- When you create groups, create them into the 2nd or 3rd bank (ID:) Leave the first bank for editorial's use.

Creating VCA groups

- Give groups clear and simple names so that you can find and use them more easily.
- Set these as Mix groups.
- After creating them, you can deactivate the groups. When deactivated, they will spill, and masters will adjust GM volume settings, but changes made to one track of a group will not change other tracks of the group.

A Tale of Two Methods

The S6 has the best of ways, and the next-best of ways to control your mix.

Attention Mode or Strip Expand Knobs? Which One Is For You?

Two powerful modalities of the S6 that users should understand are Strip Expand Knobs (Expand Knobs) mode and Attention Mode. These two features address the same needs; to give the user easier access to controls which otherwise are only reached through banking and paging in the channel strips, or, of course, VCA spill-ing. Each user will usually find that one or the other of these features appeals to their way of visualizing and focusing their workflow. For the most part, users primar-ily use only one of these features, but it is good to know them both and make an informed choice.

Strip Expand Knobs Mode – In a Nutshell

Expand Knobs mode allows users to focus their work on the fader-strip section of the console, but utilize some key features to allow quicker and simpler access to hidden controls.

Attention Mode – In a Nutshell

Attention Mode allows users to direct their work to the Attention Track fader and Touchscreen in the Master Module section of the console, accessing controls on the touch screen or its surrounding Attention Track Knobs.

While Attention Mode looks very cool in advertisements and video demos, I find that dealing with the non-tactile Touchscreen is less satisfying than using the buttons and knobs of Strip Expand mode. For me, the entire point of having a surface is to give the user a lot of different controls that can be grabbed as needed with a minimal amount of "selecting." Attention Mode is complicated and potentially confusing, takes too much time to learn, too much time to use, with too many special strokes and pokes to accomplish routine tasks. I think it will distract most users, with little return for their efforts. The Function Editor of Attention Mode does, however, give you the easiest user interface for surround panning if there is no Joystick module installed, so check that out (*see "Function Editor on page 99*).

Certainly, you may disagree. Having multiple options is one of the charms of the S6.

Expand Knobs Mode – The Simpler Way

The concept of Expand Knobs mode is that when you select a function in a track, the parameters of that function spill intelligently into the controls of the entire Knob Module, dedicating 32 knob clusters to the one active function.

Because so many parameters for a function are assigned to these physical knobs or buttons, there is far less need for banking through a function's parameters to make them available. For most common functions, all parameters are displayed at once across the controls of the Knob Module and no banking is required. When the number of parameters is larger, banking is required, but because so many parameters are displayed in each bank page, much less banking is needed.

When a function is expanded into a Knob Module, the assignment of parameters to knobs or buttons is fixed by the S6 to give consistent assignments of function parameters. For example, the **Hi-Pass Frequency In/Out** parameter of an EQ will always be assigned to the **In** button of the lower-left knob cluster, regardless of the EQ's brand or where controls for that parameter may appear on the plug-in's window of the workstation application. This uniform assignment is built into the S6[3], and in the long run makes mixing more consistent, therefore easier.

Let me expand on Expand modes

Avid has given us two different modes under the category of "Strip Expand." They are Expand Knobs and Expand Faders. Because both of these modes re-assign controls of a single channel strip across the width of a module frame, Avid assigns them a close relationship. But in actual usage, they are very far apart from one-another. I think Expand Faders are of limited value, while Expand Knobs are extremely valuable assets for every mixer.

Strip Expand Knobs mode spills plug-in (function) parameters to the 32 knobs of the Knob Module of the chassis section.

Strip Expand Faders mode spills plug-in (function) parameters to the eight faders of the chassis section.

Another mode called **Attention Expand Knobs mode** spills plug-in (function) parameters to the knobs of designated Master Knob Modules which may be anywhere on the surface. This is an advanced subject which you can explore with the Avid S6 Guide, Chapter 19.

Another great feature of Expand Knobs mode is that if the current Display Layout includes functions, the name of each parameter will appear on the display in a little "map" in the same arrangement as the knobs of the Knob Module. On the lower part of the Display Module the track name will be outlined in orange.

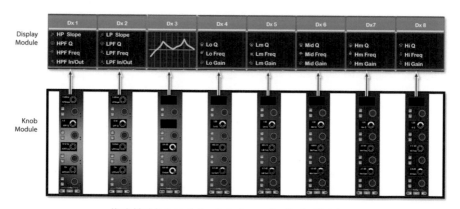

Knob Module expanded controls show on the Display Module

---

3. See Avid's S6 Guide – Appendix B for maps of EQ and Dynamics established by Avid.

If the function is a Dynamic, EQ, or Pan and has been assigned using **EQ**, **Dyn**, or **Pan** buttons on the Process section, an appropriate graph *may* be displayed on strip 3 or 8. It depends on the function's author.

To engage Expand Knobs mode:

1. Press the **Exp** button on the Process section.
   The **Exp** LED will light.
2. Choose a function on the Process Section.
3. The parameters of that function will be assigned to the entire Knob Module of that chassis section.

Top of the Process Module

While Expand Knobs mode is active, selecting any function on the Process Module buttons will send its parameters to the Knob Module and their parameter names to the Display Module.

Multiple tracks may be set to Expand mode simultaneously, but only the most recently selected track and function will be expanded to the Knob Module. The Knob Module will be re-populated when a different function or a different track is selected.

To remove a track from Expand Knobs mode do either of the following:

- Press **Exp** in that track.
- Press **Exp** on a different channel strip.

To disengage Expand Knobs mode, releasing the Knob Module, do one of these:

- Press the **Exp** button of all tracks in which its LED is lit.
- Activate **All** on the Master Module then press any lit **Exp** button.

Be sure to de-activate the **All** button afterwards.

(Note that using the **Opt/Win** modifier key does not act on the above action.)

The operation of Expand Knobs mode sounds rather complex until you use it a few times, after which it will make good sense.

Summary: All you need to do to put all the controls for a single function into the Knob Module is to press one of the function buttons on the Process Module (**Input**, **Ins**, **Send**, **Pan**, **Dyn,** or **EQ**) and then press **Exp**.

Attention Mode – The More Complicated Mode

Any single track can be *attentioned*. When attentioned, the fader section of the track is mirrored into the Attention Track Fader on the Automation Module, and the functions are assigned to the Home Screen of the Touchscreen.

When adjusting EQ, Dynamics, or Pans, a graphic image (function graph) of those functions may be displayed in the center of the Touchscreen.

Some pan adjustments may be made by touching and dragging one or two fingers on the graph of the Touchscreen, but adjustments to all other function parameters are made using the eight knobs surrounding the Touchscreen.

The process for using Attention Track mode is:

1. Attention the track.
   The fader section becomes active and functions are spilled to the Function Scroller.
2. From the Function Scroller, assign the desired EQ, Dynamic, or other function to the Function Editor.
3. Adjust the function's parameters using the Attention Track Knobs. Pans can be adjusted by touching the Touchscreen, banking them if necessary.

There are variations to the above which complicate the process, but let's start with step 1.

Attention That Track!

To attention a track do one of these:

- Press **Attention** (△) on the fader module.
- On the Home page of the Touchscreen, touch the track's icon block in the Track Scroller.
- On the Tracks page of the Touchscreen, activate the Attention button, then touch a track block in the tracks grid (*see "Attention a Track from the Tracks Screen Grid" on page 146*).

The Attention button in the channel strip is often easiest to find and use, but other options may be helpful.

The Attention button will light magenta while its track is attentioned.

To un-attention a track do one of these:

- Attention a different track.
- Press the Attention button (△) of the track, either in the Track Module or the Attention Track Fader.

Attention Track Fader Strip

When a track is attentioned, the single modifier key at the bottom will light the color of the assigned track. That key has no other purpose than to look pretty.

All other controls of the Attention Track Fader are identical to the fader section.

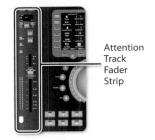

Attention Track Fader Strip

Automation Module

Root, Root, Root for the Home Screen

The Home Screen is where all the action takes place when mixing with Attention Mode. Attentioning a track usually calls up the **Home** Screen on the Touchscreen, depending on user settings. Usually the last-used parameter settings will appear on the screen.

There are two modalities of the Function Editor: Function Graphs or Parameter Banks. Function Graphs are sexier and possibly the most likely to be used, but you are more likely to see Parameter Banks in your first explorations of the Function Editor, since they are the default.

To assign the desired parameters to the Function Editor, you will need to know some module geography.

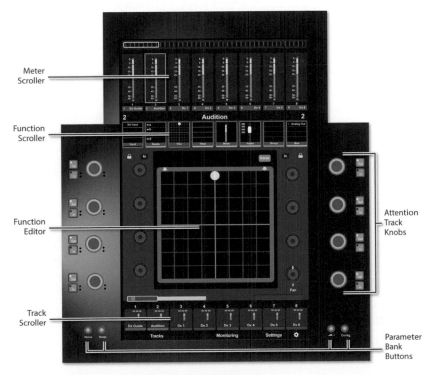

Meter Scroller

Function Scroller

Function Editor

Track Scroller

Attention Track Knobs

Parameter Bank Buttons

Home Screen and Attention Track Knobs

Attention Track Knobs

The eight knob clusters surrounding the Touchscreen are the Attention Track Knobs. They are organized into two banks: left and right. The Attention Track Knob clusters are used to adjust most function parameters. Their **In** and **Sel** buttons may alter a parameter, or may change which parameter is being adjusted, depending on the function's design.

The Function Scroller

Assigning specific functions to the temptingly large Function Editor is done using the Function Scroller, that horizontal section just above the Function Editor.

Function Blocks

The Function Scroller is populated with Function Blocks, which represent individual functions (i.e., plug-ins), function types (i.e. sends), or Function Graphs. The blocks may be color coded to indicate their function type (*see "Function Colors" on page 185*).

Swipe sideways on the Function Scroller to view all available functions, types, or graphs of the attentioned track. These blocks come in different flavors.

Graph Blocks

Fader and Meter blocks give a peek at their respective settings, but they cannot be assigned to the central Function Editor nor can they be adjusted. They are read-only.

Graph Block

The Meter block (a graph block) shows a very small meter – mostly indicating if a signal is present or not.

The fader block shows the fader position of the attentioned track, as well as the `R-I-S-M` status.

Graph Blocks for EQ, Dynamics, and Pan are explained below.

Type Block

Type Blocks

Some blocks represent types of settings, such as Sends or Inputs. These blocks will display a list of the first four parameters of their type, and when selected, the parameters will spill to the Attention Track Knobs and Function Editor in the same way that other functions spill.

Inserts Block

Inserts Block

Instead of parameters, the Inserts Block is populated with all the track's inserts. The contents of the Inserts Block may be expanded to show a single block for each insert.

Once expanded, individual functions may be selected. If the Inserts Block is touched without expanding, the inserts will be spilled to the Function Editor (and Attention Track Knobs) for individual selection.

To expand inserts in the Function Scroller, do one of these:
- Touch anywhere within the Function Scroller with two fingers, and stretch them apart, like zooming in on your smartphone.
- Touch the Inserts Block in the Function Scroller, then touch the Attention Track Knob next to the desired function, which will also assign the first plug-in to the Function Editor.

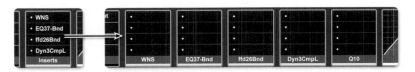

Inserts Block – collapse and expanded with finger stretch

To collapse expanded inserts:
- Touch the Function Scroller with two spread fingers, and pinch them together, like zooming out on a smartphone.

Function Editor
The most common use of the Function Editor is for adjusting EQ, Dynamics or pan parameters. When there is only one of each of these functions in a track, it is quite simple to use them; just touch the desired Function Block.

Function Graph Mode
Available for EQ, Dynamics, or Pans, a graph depicting a function may be displayed in the center of the Function Editor.

To Assign a Function Graph to the Function Editor
(When Only One of Each Type Is Instantiated):[4]
- Touch the Graphic Block – EQ, Dynamics, or Pan in the Function Scroller.

---

4. See "More on Function Graphs" on page 102 for information on using Function Graphs when multiple functions of the same type are used.

The Function Graph will spill to the Function Editor. Its first eight parameters will spill to the Attention Track Knobs. Additional parameters of the function may be banked to the Attention Track Knobs if needed (*see "Using the Bank buttons" on page 102*).

Some EQ or Dynamic plug-ins do not utilize Function Graphs.

Fader and Meter blocks display only in the Function Scroller: they cannot be moved into the Function Editor window.

Functions Without Graphs

For functions which do not utilize Function Graphs, the Function Scroller and Function Editor, or the Bank Buttons are used to select a function and assign its parameters to the Attention Track Knobs. Parameters of EQ, and Dynamics, if assigned using their Function Block instead of the Graphic Block, will also spill to the Function Editor.

To assign function parameters to the Function Editor:

- Touch the desired Function Block in the Function Scroller.

All parameters of a function are pre-assigned to groups of four Parameter Banks. Banks may be assigned to either the left or right Attention Track Knobs using either the Bank Buttons or the Function Editor.

The first two Parameter Banks of the selected function are assigned to the left and right Attention Track Knobs.

If the desired parameters of the function appear on the Attention Track Knobs, you are ready to adjust! If not, you must get them assigned to the knobs.

Assigning Parameter Blocks to Attention Track Knobs Using the Touchscreen

This method gives you more direct control but requires more study of the system.

The Function Editor displays a grid of Parameter Banks for the selected function. The grid is vague and sometimes appears haphazard because some banks have fewer than four parameters each.

The grid shows the banks stacked two high and eight across, lit in their function color. The two assigned parameter groups have large brackets; left brackets pointing to left-knob assignment, right brackets pointing to right-knob assignments.

Swiping within the window will reveal additional Parameter Banks, if any.

Group Block Selection

If a Group Block was selected from the Function Scroller, the first eight functions in that group are assigned to the Attention Track Knobs. When a Group Block contains more than eight functions, overflow functions will be assigned to parameter blocks. These may be assigned to the Attention Track Knobs, adding an extra step to parameter assignment.

To select a function from a Group Block:

- Press the Attention Track Knob of the desired function.

Parameter Banks in the Function Editor

The Function Editor may be swiped sideways to reveal additional banks.

To assign Parameter Banks to Attention Track Knobs using the Touchscreen:

1. In the Function Scroller, touch the desired function.
2. Touch and hold the desired parameter bank in the Function Editor.
   a. Brackets will slowly flash around the selected parameter bank.
   b. The brackets will continue to flash for only a few seconds.
3. Touch any Attention Track Knob on the right or left side of the Touchscreen. The parameter bank will be assigned to knobs on that side.

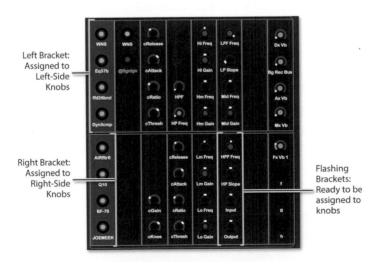

Parameter groups in the Function Editor

To assign Parameter Banks to Attention Track Knobs using the Bank buttons:

Parameter Bank buttons

- While holding down the **mmShift** button, press one of the banking buttons below the Attention Track Knobs.
  - ○ **Home** and **Swap** buttons bank the left side Attention Track Knobs left or right.
  - ○ **Back** (◢▬▬◣) and **Config** buttons bank the right-side Attention Track Knobs left or right.
  - ○ When the same function is assigned to both sides, all eight Attention Track Knobs will bank regardless of which side's Bank Buttons are used.

Lock Those Knobs

The left and right Attention Track Knob banks may be locked to Parameter Banks of a function. The knobs remain assigned to that parameter bank regardless of the function which has been called to the Function Editor.

Home Screen

To lock or unlock Attention Track Knobs:

- Touch the padlock icon at the top corner of the of the Function Editor.

When the padlock is lit the Attention Track Knobs will maintain this assignment until they are unlocked.

> You might imagine that this could cause you all sorts of confusion if you inadvertently toggle the lock, or if you forget that you have locked those knobs. It is something to keep in mind as you are using the Function Editor.

More on Function Graphs

Where more than one EQ or Dynamics plug-in is instantiated in a track, the last-focused plug-in will be recalled when the Function Graph is selected in the Function Scroller.

To assign a different EQ or Dynamic function to the Function Graph, do one of these:

- On the DAW screen, select the desired plug-in.
- On the Process Section of the attentioned track, double-press the EQ or Dyn button to cycle through desired functions.

Pertinent settings for Function Graph use

Two settings to explore if you are interested in using the Function Graphs are:

- **Home Screen > Local Settings (✿)/Auto Show Function Graph on Selection** When set on, automatically shows the Function Graph of EQ, Dynamics, or Pan when a track is enabled.
- **Home Screen > Home Screen > Local Settings (✿)/Auto Show Function Graph on Knob Touch** Temporarily shows the Function Graph of any function when its knob is adjusted. The graph stays on screen for up to 5 seconds, depending on this setting. Set to "0" to disable this feature.

Additional controls on the Home Screen

Above and below the central Function Editor on the Home Screen are the Meter Scroller and the Track Scroller.

Swipe the Meter Scroller (or the Meter Universe) to scroll through the input meters of all visible tracks in the open session.

Swipe the Track Scroller (or the Track Universe) to scroll through icon blocks representing each visible track currently on the surface. The function of the Track Scroller changes when in Assign mode, and it becomes the Strip Scroller, where Layouts are assembled in the process of creating them *(see "Creating Track Layouts" on page 140).*

Tapping the icon in a Meter or Track scroller may attention its track, depending on preference settings.

A Home Screen Local setting can lock the Meter and Track scrollers together so that scrolling one will scroll the other. *That should be the default, but it isn't.*

Universe bars

Universe Views

Above the Meter Scroller and the Track Scroller areas of the Function Editor screen are two truncated bars which are Universe Views. The width of the window represents a proportional model of all the tracks in the session. A framed window in the bar indicates the section of the universe which is currently visible in the scroller. Touching in the universe bar or touch-dragging the framed window scrolls the framed tracks into view in the track or Meter Scroller.

A great feature of the Meter Universe bar is that it is made up of tiny little functioning meters. They are too small to read, but they could be extremely helpful if you are searching out a signal that is somewhere within a large session. Every un-hidden track is represented in the universe bar. You can drag the framed window over any little meters which are firing and immediately display them in the scroller bar below. Maybe one of them is the track you seek.

In summary, I think that when using Attention Mode the user would spend far more time swiping and searching in scrollers and with display modes and selections, than with actual mixing. The exception is that when working with surround-format mixes, the Function Editor is the best tool for panning.

Chapter 9

Ready for Mixing at a Basic Level

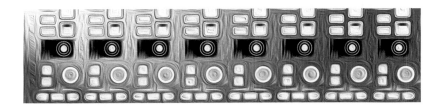

We have come a long way since sitting down at the S6, so let us look at what has been covered and the relevance to mixing a real project.

To mix outside the DAW window and down on the S6 surface, you have mastered the basic controls of the channel strips.

Banking

Many people lose their way (and cannot find their tracks) when they do not understand the Banking paradigm of the S6. Becoming stuck inadvertently in Layout Mode has stymied many users but recognizing modes which we have not yet investigated allows you to bypass them and get on with your work.

Understanding Banking controls allows you to move desired tracks to within your reach.

The **User 1** and **User 2** modifier keys help you with simplicity. More sweeping banking controls are at your command on the Master Module.

Transport and Locations

The position of the playhead in the timeline is under your control. The standard transport buttons of Play, Stop, and Fast Forward, are good for nearby playing, recording, and reviewing. Audio recording can be punched in and out from transport buttons as well.

Jumping to specific timeline positions can be accomplished with the locate buttons. Pressing the star allows you to jump to an exact frame.

Get used to the **Jump Back**, **Jump Forward**, and **Loop Toggle** transport buttons, as they are a great help when auditioning your mix adjustments.

DOI: 10.4324/9781003111801–11

Faders

Nearly all the functions of the faders have been covered. There are some additional features that can be called from the faders, but volume control, automation mode control, track information can all be controlled or monitored in the fader section.

Functions: Plug-ins and Sends

Using the Process Section to spill functions to the knob modules, and the ability to navigate within a knob section to display a desired parameter puts every parameter into your fingers. This access is comparable to most modern digital cinema mix consoles. To adjust a send, press Sends and grab the send you need in the Knob Section. To adjust an EQ, press EQ, then nudge the Knob Section to the parameter and tweak it. Every function of a track can be called up with just a few button pushes.

Automation

When you have configured the Display Module to show automation data, you have the super-power to display the data of any control by simply touching that control while holding **Ctrl + Opt/Win** on the modifier keys.

Switching from one automation mode to another is easily accomplished with the F button and can be multiplied by the **Opt/Win** or **Shift + Opt/Win** modifier keys.

A QuickJump (**Shift + 0**) assigns automation pages to the Master Module Soft Key pads which give you shortcut buttons to automation mode assignments and preview features which enhance your mixing power significantly.

Display

With control over the format of the track displays in the Display Modules, track names, audio levels, function graphs, clip names, waveforms, automation data and more can be shown as the session plays. Tracks can be configured individually or globally. Meters can be configured to different sizes, types and standards, and they may be locked in place to act as sub-master or master meters.

How Do You Mix on the Surface?

The first time I sat down to mix on a brand-new Icon D-Control, I asked the sales representative who was there to help us get up and running, "How do you mix on this thing?"

He told me about a great feature called "Glide to All Enabled."

"That's nice, but how do I mix on this?"

He demonstrated how to display track numbers in the scribble strips.

"What I mean is, how do I audition a clip, adjust the level, adjust the EQ, adjust the pan, add some reverb, apply all of those adjustments to a string of clips and play it back to see how it sounds?"

He looked unsettled but said "You hit Play and adjust the knobs."

"But then I am writing automation of my adjustments as I make them. Even if I reach a setting I like before reaching the end of the clip, it won't be applied to the entire clip," I said. "Isn't there some method for doing that?"

He told me that he had shown a lot of people all the features of the D-Control, but no one had ever asked him that.

Let me give you a quick little description of how you can use this S6 to mix your project. If you already know how, there is no shame in jumping to the next chapter, where more of the fun features of the S6 will be discussed.

How I Mix on the Surface

Let us take the example of pre-mixing some dialog and sound effects.

The first part of the task is to create the mix template, and while that could possibly be done on the S6, I would do it in Pro Tools.

Without getting into the details and naming conventions, sequence of plug-ins, track colors and so on, let me give the hypothetical particulars of this session. This is intended only as an example of mixing process, not template building.[1]

This is a 5.1 session with mono source tracks which have plug-ins installed and sends to multiple dialog or effects reverb busses. When multi-track audio is presented it is placed into contiguous mono tracks.

There is a set each of reverb aux tracks for dialog and for effects. Their inputs come from either the dialog or effects source track sends. Those sends are defaulted to Mute On and send level to unity, which allows me to open a send by simply toggling the send mute.

Dialog and effects each have a sub-master aux track which feeds a stem record track, which feeds the print master record track. The sub-masters have EQ and compressors instantiated.

---

1. For details see "Details of example in Chapter 9" on page 209.

The template was built with neutral default automation setting breakpoints anchored just ahead of the head pop. Mute is left un-anchored because I do not want to write mute automation. Source clips were dropped into tracks with "automation follows edit" disabled, so I have a clean slate ahead.

VCA Masters top the session: Dx VCA, Fx VCA, Stems VCA. The source tracks and their respective reverb aux tracks are members of the first two VCA groups; Stems and Print Master record tracks in the third. If the effects were very wide, I might create VCA sub-masters for Hard FX, BGs, and Foley, grouped under the Fx VCA Master.

On the surface, I set the Display Layout of the three multi-channel record tracks to Large Meter and set their type in Pro Tools to K-20.

Being sure that the surface is in Banking mode, I bank those four record tracks to the right-most positions on the surface and lock them there. This gives me a stable meter set, showing all three stems and the printmaster.

I press **Shift + 1** to place automation pages into all four Soft Key pads, and check **Automation 3** SoftKey page to see that the automation types are to my liking. I disable **Mute Enable**, as I do not want to write Mute automation.

I press **Opt/Win + Touch** (**Automation 1** soft key page) to put all tracks into Touch mode which is my "normal" mix mode.

I play through the first scene and get some sense of levels and other needs, and then begin at the start, taking on dialog.

With the surface in Banking mode and banked all the way to the left, the VCA Masters take up the first three tracks. Pressing **Menu + right** on the VCA Master, the dialog tracks are spilled to the right of the VCA Master.

The first clip is very low, so before making any adjustments, I check the monitor section of the Master Module to be sure that volume is set to -0.0 and that **Dim** is not selected. I would have already checked this setting, but it is judicious to check again at this early point.

I want to get a good setting of volume, EQ, and dialog processing for the first clip, so I activate Preview on the Automation 2 page of the Soft Key pad and play through the clip, making adjustments to those controls. After some level adjustment, there is a peak in the middle of the clip that is too loud, but the rest is good.

The dialog in the clip is a bit dull, so I press EQ in the Process Section to call an EQ to the Knob Section. Because both the EQ 3 and the SA2 are considered by Avid to be EQs, their names appear in the Knob Section. I press the EQ3 knob and its first four parameters appear. Using the nudge (▶) button at the bottom of the Knob Section, I navigate to the HMF control to the Knob Section and make the adjustments.

(The alternative to fooling with the navigation buttons of the Knob Section is to activate Expand Knobs mode to spill all the parameters of the EQ3 to the Knob Module (*see "Expand Knobs Mode" on page* 93). Press **Exp** in the Process Section to toggle Expand Knob mode. Press **All** and then **Exp** and all tracks will be set to Expand Knobs mode.)

The clip needs a bit of room reverb to give it a better feeling of the environment, so I press **Sends** on the Process Section. In the Knob Section I press the **In**-button on the chosen send to un-mute it, sending the audio to its reverb. I hear the reverb immediately, and it is too loud.

Looking at the surface I can see that the reverb aux track is not being displayed, so I press **User 2** modifier key until the reverb track is visible. I lower aux track's output to a better level. I want to tweak the reverb's size setting, so I press **Ins** in the Process Section of reverb aux. There is only one reverb plug-in in this aux, so the reverb parameters spill to the Knob Section, or if Expand Knobs is still active, the parameters all spill to the Knob Module. After adjusting the size setting, I bank back to the source track using **User 1**.

(When building the session, I could have created Dx reverb VCA and Fx reverb VCA Masters, with their respective reverb aux tracks as their respective GMs, then spilled reverbs to the surface.)

When I am satisfied that I have a good overall setting for this clip, I move the insertion point to just ahead of the clip by holding the ◀◀ button on the transport keys, press **Play** and press **Punch Preview** on the Soft Key pad. Automation begins writing all the parameter adjustments that I made to the dialog tracks, the reverb aux level, and the reverb plug-in's size setting. Writing continues until I press **Stop** on the transport.

Having already listened through the scene I know that this same shot was used twice more. Since the settings remain in the Preview Buffer, I fast-forward to the next clip from that source and listen to it. If it seems appropriate, I might back up to the start of that clip and press **Play**, then **Punch Preview** again to write the settings to that clip, and possibly the next as well.

Using ◀◀ I return to the first clip. It needs a little dip at a loud point in the middle. I check the OLED of that track to assure that automation is still in **Touch** mode, then play forward and try to dip the fader at just the right point. Doh! I dipped too much and too late, so I press **Undo** on the Master Module, and try again, repeating until it sounds good. Now on to the next clip…

After spilling and/or banking, the contents of the surface may become messy. It is very easy to return the surface to "Home" position by pressing **mmShift + Home**. Touch the lit **Menu** button of any VCA Master or GM to unspill that VCA group. Two buttons to restore order.

That is pretty much it. I use Preview extensively to get overall audio settings because it absorbs changes made to all tracks and functions at once. I can punch the same Preview settings into multiple timeline locations and not have to worry about which tracks to select. It is possible to save Preview settings as Snapshots and recall them later, but I rarely find the need to do so (*see "Snapshots" on page* 171).

I spill and unspill the VCA Masters to bring desired groups of tracks to the surface. Remember that a track can be a member of more than one VCA group, so some important tracks can show up on multiple VCA spills.

Some people prefer to use the Attention mode to adjust parameters in the Function Editor of the Touchscreen rather than using Expand Knobs mode. Try it each way, see which you like best.

In upcoming chapters we will find some much better tools to optimize your workflow and do greater and more interesting things in less time and with less effort.

This is a good start.

Part III

Intermediate Tools

Chapter 10
More Advanced Features

More Fun Ahead

From this point onward we get to explore some of the more interesting and often help-ful features of the S6.

Do to All, Do to Selected

Sometimes you want to change a setting on some or all tracks in a session. S6 and Pro Tools have a couple of ways to accomplish this. These commands can be applied to all tracks or selected tracks:

Do To All (or Selection) Using Option Modifier Key

Do to All   Do to Selected

Modifier Keys

This works on **Select**, **Mute**, **Solo**, **Record**, **Input**, **Send Mute**, plug-in bypass, and setting automation modes, making I/O assignments, instantiating plug-ins, and instantiating sends.

Using Modifiers

- Hold **Opt** while applying a command to apply the command to all tracks.
- Hold **Opt + Shift** while applying a command will apply it to all *selected* tracks.
- Hold **Opt + Shift + Command** while selecting an I/O assignment will cascade selections to all selected tracks, beginning from the chosen I/O path, and cycling through path assignments until all selected tracks are assigned (*see "Cascading Outputs" on page 202 for more details*).

Using the All Button on the Master Module

The **All** button affects Process selections in the Process section (**Ins**, **Pan**, **Sends**, **Dyn**, **EQ**, etc.), and Expand mode.

DOI: 10.4324/9781003111801–13

Do To All using the All button:

1. Press the **All** button on the Lower Master Module.
2. Select any mode on the Process section of any track.
   a. All tracks will be set to the selected mode.

The **All** mode remains active until toggled off.

Another **Do To All/Do To Selected** method is available when using automation pages of Soft Key pads (*see "Using Do To All or Do To Selected in Soft Key pad" on page 58 for more information*).

PEC/Direct – Monitoring After and Before the Recorder

For cinema mixing, we are usually recording the stems on an early pass through the mix, then going back repeatedly to make changes in our mix, punching into and out of audio record mode. This gives us a lot of flexibility while mixing. For example, if the dialog stem has already been recorded through a scene and editorial changes need to be done somewhere in that reel or project, the dialog stem may be set to playback (PEC), and the dialog source may be taken off-line, but the music and effects can continue to be mixed, listening to the recorder's playback of the dialog. After changes to the off-line dialog are complete, it is put back online, and the dialog monitor set to Direct, ready to do more mixing changes.

Standard Style

PEC/Direct Style

Input vs PEC/Direct

At the point in the timeline where we punch in and out of record on a stem or master, we want the levels to match between what is already recorded (PEC[1]) and the input to the recorder (Direct). If they do not match at those two points, there will be a jump in the mix levels, which is undesirable. To determine if our levels are matching, we play through our in- and out-points and toggle the PEC/Direct switch, listening carefully for a good match. If all is good, we jump back, play through, and punch the recorder in and out at the right moments.

On most cinema mix desks, the PEC/Direct switch indicates its state by a colored light within the switch. The standard is that the switch lights green when in PEC, and it lights white when monitoring Direct. When Pro Tools was first designed, they called this switch the Input switch. When in direct (input) it is green and when in playback (PEC) it is white, the opposite of film industry standards. To calm the complaints from film mixers and engineers, Avid added an optional feature in **Setup/**

---

1. PEC stands for Photo Electric Cell. It is a 1930s legacy term referring to the monitoring of optically recorded audio. For now, PEC means Playback.

`Preferences/Operation/Record` called `PEC/Direct  Style  Input Monitoring`. When selected, the `Input` button on all tracks changes to `P` (Green) or `D` (Gray) for PEC or Direct. The S6 Post Module features dedicated PEC/Direct switches which adhere to the cinema standard.

Knob Control Displays
All the Knobs Look Alike – Well, Sort Of…

Although at first glance all the knobs do look alike, the S6 OLEDs and other displays show them differently depending on their function. There are different ways knob displays can look. If you know their function, you may be better able to identify the one you are trying to grab.

1. **Level** – The bright mark on a **Level** control represents a Level setting. Fully counter-clockwise is -∞, and fully clockwise is +12.

Knob controls displays

2. **Width** – The bright marks on a **Width** display represent the amount of width, spreading outward symmetrically from top center (no width) to 5:00 and 7:00 (full width). This is typically used in Q settings in EQ plug-ins

3. **Plus-Minus** – The bright marks on a **Plus-Minus** (sometimes called Cut-Boost) display shows a lowering (cut) of signal counter-clockwise from the top center, or a raising (boost) of signal clockwise from the top center. This would typically be used for the gain level on an EQ, since it can represent both negative and positive values.

4. **Position** – The bright mark on a **Position** knob shows a "low vs. high" or a "left vs. right" position, used in pans or frequency adjustments. Left or low are at 7:00, high or right at 5:00, center or midway at 12:00.

5. The center circle of a knob display sometimes indicates whether the parameter is active or bypassed. Sometimes it indicates a control state, such as an EQ's type.

Chapter 11

Soft Keys – Shortcuts to Commands

The many commands and settings of the S6 and the DAW may be scattered where they are difficult to access. One of the unique features of the S6, Soft Keys, opens some windows into those tools, putting commands closer to your fingertips. I do not know if "Power User" is still a thing, but Soft Keys bring you closer to being an S6 Power User.

Intro to Soft Keys

Back in Chapter 6 we learned how to set the automation mode of one or more tracks using the Soft Key pads, but there is much more to Soft Key pads than that (*see "Prepare to set automation mode using a Soft Key pad" on page 58 to review*).

Soft Keys offer shortcuts which allow you to execute commands of the S6 or the workstation(s), or to navigate to other Soft Key pages. They are rather like the F-Keys on the Pro Tools keyboard.

Some Soft Keys are essential to your efficient operation of the S6. Some are helpful, giving you another access point for a button that may be hard to reach. MANY of the Soft Keys simply offer an alternative way to apply settings and modes that might be more easily done on the workstation screen. You must, however, have some understanding of how to control Soft Keys.

Collections of Soft Keys are organized into pages of 12 Soft Key commands. The pages can be assigned to what Avid calls Soft Key banks. *To avoid confusion with other kinds of banks or banking, I will refer to these as Soft Key pads.*

A Soft Key Pad

A Soft Key pad consists of a small screen with six selection buttons on each side, and three navigation buttons below. Two Soft Key pads are built into the Lower Master Module, and two into the Automation Module.

DOI: 10.4324/9781003111801–14

Soft Key Pages

Soft key pages each have a name in a color-coded banner at the top, 12 related Soft Keys in two columns, and three navigation choices across the bottom. If a page has more than one bank of Soft Keys, subsequent banks are also called pages. Thus, there is **Automation 1**, **Automation 2**, etc. You can usually navigate between banks (pages) of the same page type using the navigation buttons at the bottom of the pad. If there is a **Home** key on the bottom of a page, it will return to the first bank of that page.

An Easy Path to Useful Soft Key Pages

By default, the S6 assigns some good pages to the Soft Key pads, but if a stray button push has moved them, you will want to get back to a starting point quickly. Poking around on the navigation keys can be ineffective. Happily, Avid has provided an easy way to get you back on track.

To get some useful automation Soft Key pages onto the pads quickly:

- Hold **Shift** modifier key and press **0** on the numeric keypad.

This is called a QuickJump, and it assigns one of 14 configurations of Soft Key pages to the four Soft Key pads. It takes two hands to accomplish a QuickJump, since you need to hold that **Shift** modifier key, way over there in the left-most channel strip of the nearest fader section, while you press one of the QuickJump selector keys, which inhabit the numeric keypad *and beyond* (*see "QuickJump to Soft Key pages" on page 121 for a list of the QuickJumps and their content*). We will dig deeper into Soft Key pads in the next chapter.

Using Soft Key Pads
Soft Key Pads, Pages, Shortcuts and Appsets

As discussed earlier, Soft Keys are shortcut keys collected onto pages and displayed onto Soft Key pads, which have buttons that trigger or apply the Soft Key shortcuts.

Appsets

Soft Key pages can be created or edited at the user's whim,[1] saved as collections called appsets (application sets), then recalled. Avid endeavors to make the S6 work with several different brands of workstations; creating appsets for the different menu

---

1. See Avid's S6 Guide: SoftKeys Editor for a thorough understanding of appsets.

choices of different DAWs works towards that goal. Avid provides a default appset for Pro Tools, so that's what we will cover at this time (*for help in using or building your own custom appsets, see Chapter 8 of Avid's S6 Guide*).

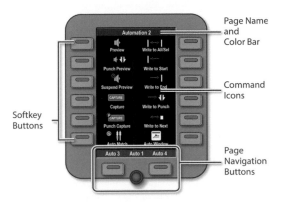

Soft Key pad (aka Soft Key bank)

Soft Key shortcuts execute actions, toggle modes, make selections, adjust settings, and do nearly anything within the Pro Tools or S6 software universe. The combination of a hardware button with a graphic icon makes these 48 buttons powerful tools –*if* you can get the desired page assigned to a Soft Key pad.

Once located, Soft Key shortcuts are quite easy to use – you push the button for the command that you want to trigger. Some shortcuts are momentary; others toggle on and off. Sometimes you must hold the button down while selecting a track or touching a control on the surface.

Some active mixing controls, such as **Preview**, **Write to…**, and **Memory Locations** are not available on the surface. These are the controls that are the most useful to get onto the Soft Key pads. Pages in the Pro Tools appset are built and ready to go.

For S6 settings that you use many times each day, the Soft Keys are very helpful. For less frequently used S6 settings, it may be faster and easier to use the settings pages of the Touchscreen. If you are proficient with Pro Tools you could be better off using the Pro Tools interface for settings and adjustments with which you are already comfortable.

S6 demos and sales materials give a lot of attention to user-customized Soft Key pages. There are some instances where it is worth the time and effort required to create custom pages, but I suggest that new users learn what they can of the Pro Tools appset, before investing their time and energy managing custom pages.

The default appset (Pro Tools) should appear at startup, displaying the following pages onto the four pads: **Automation 1**, **Session Management 1**, **Automation 2**, and **Extras 1.** This is the default, and it can always be retrieved with the QuickJump 0 (**Shift + 0** on numerical keypad of the Master Module).

These Soft Key pages have some useful choices, but you may want to summon different pages to Soft Key pads for your different needs.

What Page Is It On?

Navigating to the desired page of Soft Keys within an appset can sometimes be challenging. Some non-Soft Key actions cause dedicated pages to pop up, displacing desired pages. There is no clear map which shows how to navigate to a particular page. I will try to describe how to navigate a pad to a page. This gets messy, but fear not! There is an alternative method which may prove easier, but it is good for you to first have some understanding of manual navigation within Soft Key pages.

Navigating to Soft Key Pages Manually

At the top of each page is a color-coded title bar with the name of that page, which briefly describes its content. Unfortunately, the color coding of the bars is a bit flexible. Some colors are used for different page types. For example, Machine Control pages and Satellite are both gray. So let's just count on the colors giving us something to recognize when we reach for the Soft Key button.

Strange Factoid

On the **Automation 1** SoftKey page, any automation modes which are currently active on any track(s) in a session will be highlighted. This does not tell us which or how many tracks may be set to one mode or another, only that one or more tracks are set to such mode. Is that helpful?

Soft Key Pad Navigation Buttons

At the bottom of each page is a gray bar with three navigation labels for the buttons below. *Often* the center button navigates to a previous page, or sometimes it closes the current page or group of pages, or sometimes it just navigates to a different, related page. It depends. *Often* the other two buttons navigate to a different, related page. Do not expect that you will always be able to navigate back to the previous page. If you see a desired page on the navigation buttons, *great!* If you do not, you may poke around and maybe find it.

Alternate Soft Key Page Choices

To make matters more interesting, pressing the **Ctrl** modifier key will sometimes swap the three navigation choices for another layer of navigation choices, or alternate choices will appear on the page. Surprise!! You never know what you will find. For example, if you are looking at the **Automation 2** page, the normal navigation choices are **Auto 3**, **Auto 1**, and **Auto 4**. Hold down **Ctrl** and the choices change to **AutoSpec**, **Snaps**, and **Auto Prefs.** These are intended to be shortcuts, I think.

But Wait – There's More!

Pressing the **WS**, **Layout Mode,** or **Type** buttons on the Master Module will call their respective Soft Key pages to the Master Module Soft Key pads. These pages are persistent; they will latch onto a Soft Key pad and not relinquish it until **Close** is selected on the pad. If you forget about this feature it can drive you crazy when you need to get **Automation 1** onto the Soft Key pad but **Layouts** stubbornly remains there.

Isn't There an Easier Way to Find my Soft Key Pages?

Yes! QuickJump!

QuickJump is an S6 feature which applies one of 16 collections of Soft Key pages to the Soft Key pads, activated by shortcut keys. **Shift** (modifier key) plus one of the following keys will call up standard and stable Soft Key pages.

Note that firmware versions 2019.5 and 2018.3 are slightly different.

QuickJump to Soft Key Pages

Table 11.1 QuickJump destinations for Pro Toolsv2019.5 Appset

Keys	Name	Description
Shift + 0	Default	The default Soft Key pages Automation 1, Session Management 1, Automation 2, and Extras 1.
Shift + 1	Automation	Automation pages 1–4.
Shift + 2	Automation Alt 1	Automation pages 1 and 2 on the Automation Module Soft Key pads (useful when Layouts are shown in both the left and right Soft Key pads).

(Continued)

Table 11.1 (Continued)

Keys	Name	Description
Shift + 3	Automation Alt 2	Automation page 1 on the right Master Module Soft Key Pad (useful when Layouts are shown on only the left Pad).
Shift + 4	Management	Session management pages on all Pads.
Shift + 5	Satellites & Machines	All four Pads display pages for Satellites, Machine Control, Solo (SIP/AFL/PFL, and switch behavior), and more.
Shift + 6	Configuration Editor	Interface, Tools and Setup, Session Management 1, and Counters and Scrolling pages appear on the four pads.
Shift + 7	Editing	Pages and commands to edit Clips, Clip Gain, Clip FX, Selections, and Tracks.
Shift + 8	MIDI	MIDI composition, creation, and editing commands.
Shift + 9	Recording	Commands for recording, tracking, and Playlists.
Shift +.(decimal)	Monitoring	Access control room Sources and Speakers, toggle Sum/Inter-cancel modes. Fold-downs, Talkback, Listenback, and Monitoring Preferences.
Shift + Enter	Zone Banking	Bank, Nudge, Home, and End for each Spill Zone (Left and Right). *These pages give you direct control of all banking.*
Shift + /	Track and Meters	Track and Meter Layouts.
Shift + *	Preferences	Console Preferences.
Mem Loc	Memory Locations	All Soft Key pads allocated to Memory Locations. (Shift key not required).

Table 11.2 Pro Tools Appset differences in v2018.3

Keys	Name	Description
Shift + /	User Pages	Blank User Page 2 into lower-right Key Pad, gives easy access to User pages 1 and 3. Page 3 is nearly identical to Automation 2, but it has **Save** button.
Shift + *	Preferences	Frequently used S6 Preference settings populate Soft Key pads.

(A printable version of this table can be found on page 228.)

Page Menu

On the default **Automation 1** page is a Soft Key called **Page Menu** which brings up a selection of 12 other interesting pages. One of these may be what you are seeking, or it may be related to the page you need. From there you may learn where to find a desired page. Or maybe you won't.

Some Soft Key Page Suggestions

Two very helpful pages you will need to use are **Automation 1** and **Automation 2**, which show up in the two left Soft Key Pads of the QuickJump **Shift + 0.**

Keys on **Automation 1** allow you to directly set the automation mode of one or more tracks without cycling through the modes.

Keys on **Automation 2** give the user surface access to **Preview**, **Suspend Preview**, **Punch Preview,** and **Write to...** commands. These are essential for mixing.

Mode-Specific Pages

As previously mentioned, pressing **WS**, **Layout Mode**, or **Type** will assign Soft Key pages to the pad of the Lower Master Module.
- Press **Layout Mode**: select from a list of Track Layouts.
- Press **WS**: easily focus workstations or check the designation status of workstations and applications. Press **mmShift + WS** to open the Workstations page on the Touchscreen at the same time.
- Press **Type**: select from a list of tracks to assign to the mixing surface.

If you have time, bump around in the Soft Keys sections and find some treasures of your own. Be sure you remember how you got to them.

Chapter 12

Spill Zones – What, Why, and Where Are They?

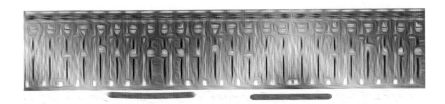

What Are Spill Zones?

You are the Emperor of Mixing. You want to proclaim a special group of channel strips as your personal "special place" on the S6 surface. Here, you can command collections of tracks such as automobiles, dog barks, or reverb returns, to appear. You can even command tracks from a chosen workstation to appear here. While your special place is active, the rest of the surface behaves as if your special place has a castle wall around it. It is somewhat magic, so it can disappear in an instant and the other tracks won't even realize that something has changed. Your Special Place is the Spill Zones.

The S6 allows users to designate up to two groups of channel strips to be Spill Zones. When Spill Zone channel strips are occupied, they are exempted from the standard banking mode. Groups of tracks (track groups) may be assigned (spilled) into one of the Spill Zones.

The track groups which may be spilled are: VCA's, Layouts, Tracks by Type, and Tracks by Workstation. It is also possible to spill selected tracks to a Spill Zone, though doing so is a bit more complicated.

The two Spill Zones are labeled **Left Spill** and **Right Spill**. It is therefore sensible to configure strips on the left side of the console as Left Spill, and those on the right as Right Spill. Users who want to be eccentric may do otherwise.

Spill Zones displace the tracks which were otherwise assigned to those channel strips. The width of the Spill Zone is variable; it will be no wider than the number of tracks designated, or the number of tracks spilled, whichever is smaller. For example, if a Spill Zone is configured to be 12 channels wide and an eight-channel layout is

DOI: 10.4324/9781003111801-15

spilled into it, only eight tracks on the surface will be displaced. If a 15-track layout is spilled into a 12-track wide Spill Zone, the tracks must be banked or banked within the 12-track Spill Zone to show them.

A Note on VCA Spilling

Earlier, we explore VCA spilling, which is sometimes *involved* with Spill Zones, but is not the same thing (*see "Spilling VCA Masters" on page 86*).

What is important to note is that when VCA spilling is active, it takes possession of some of the channel strips of the S6 surface. Normal banking takes place around spilled VCA tracks. So, when I refer to "normal banking" I mean "banking tracks which are not possessed by VCA spill tracks."

Cut to the Chase: Spill Zones
How Do Spill Zones Work?

1. Configure the Spill Zones: designate which channel strips of the surface you want to be the Spill Zones (*see "Configuring Spill Zones" below*).
2. Activate a Spill Zone: press **L Spill** or **R Spill** buttons.
3. Spill tracks into the Spill Zone by pressing **Layout Mode**, **Type**, or **WS** on the Master Module.
4. Select desired group on the Soft Key pad.
5. To unspill: press **mmShift** + **L Spill** or **R Spill** or press a colored **Menu** button on one of the spilled tracks.

Configuring Spill Zones

Configuring Spill Zones designates which strips comprise each Spill Zone. It is easy to configure Spill Zones. Remember, however, that Spill Zone settings are saved in the system settings, so they may not be saved with your session. You can configure the Title settings to include the Spill Zone State.

To configure Spill Zones:

1. Navigate to **Settings** > **Surface** > **Config** on the Touchscreen.

The Spill Zone Configuration will appear on the touchscreen, with current Spill Zones indicated by purple strips along the bottom.

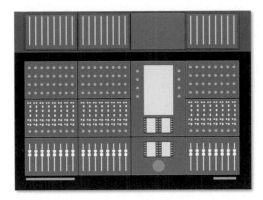

Violet bars below faders indicate Spill Zone locations

2. Select **L Spill** or **R Spill** on the bottom of the configuration screen.
   On the surface, the Attention (△) buttons of all strips in the selected Spill Zone will light.
3. On the surface, press the Attention (△) button of the first channel that you want to designate to the Spill Zone.
4. On the surface, press the Attention (△) button of the last track that you want to designate to the Spill Zone.
   The purple strip will indicate the new selection.
5. Use **Undo**, **Clear**, or **Cancel** if needed.
6. Press **Done** to save the displayed Spill Zone.

Repeat as often as you like.

Using Spill Zones

Controls for the Spill Zones are in the Locations section of the Lower Master Module. The **L Spill** and **R Spill** buttons give more information than action. We will start with the actions.

Spill Button Actions

The only actions you can take with an L Spill or R Spill button are:

- Activating that Spill Zone – setting it as the target of any spilling.
- Assigning banking buttons so that they bank within that Spill Zone.
- Unspilling the Spill Zone.

Spill Zone controls

To spill selected tracks into a Spill Zone:
1. Navigate the Touchscreen to the Tracks Screen.
2. Press **L Spill** or **R Spill** button on the Lower Master Module.
3. Touch `Assign` on the Tracks Screen.
4. In the track matrix, touch to select the tracks that you want to spill.
   - Selected tracks will become outlined in green.
   - Touching selected tracks again will de-select them.
5. On the Touchscreen, touch **Spill**.

If the width of spilled tracks is greater than the active Spill Zone, the Bank and Nudge button LEDs will light with the element color.

To spill Track Layouts, track types, or Workstations into a Spill Zone:
1. Press **L Spill** or **R Spill** button on the Lower Master Module
   - This "enables" the zone.
   - The LED will light white (bright blue).
2. Press **Layout Mode**, **WS**, or **Type** button on the Lower Master Module to select the desired track type.
3. In a Soft Key pad, select the desired Track Layout, Workstation, or Track Type.
   - Those tracks will spill into the Zone.
   - The Spill LED will light the element color (*see "Bank and Nudge Switch Element Colors" on page 186*).
   - On the surface the **Menu** button LEDs of spilled tracks will light the element color.

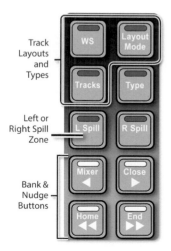

Track Layouts and Types

Left or Right Spill Zone

Bank & Nudge Buttons

Master Module Spill/Bank buttons

To bank within a Spill Zone:
- Press **L Spill** or **R Spill** button to select which zone to bank.

  The LED will light white (bright blue).

  If there are bankable tracks in the Spill Zone, the **B&N** button LEDs will light the element color.
- Use the **Bank** and **Nudge** buttons to bank within that Spill Zone.

  If **B&N** buttons are not lit, there are no tracks to bank.

To clear Spill Zones
The state of a Spill Zone cannot be temporarily disabled, then re-enabled. Elements are either spilled into a spill zone, or the Spill Zone is empty (disabled).

Unspilling (referred to in the S6 settings as *collapsing*) returns the Spill Zone channel strips to the console at large.

To unspill a Spill Zone do one of the these:
- Press **mmShift + L Spill** or **R Spill** buttons.
- Press any lit **Menu** button on a Spill Zone channel strip.

User Settings
There are quite a few settings for Spill Zones. Under **User Settings**, check **Banking**, **Attention**, and **Strips** sections.

Hobo Signs – Deciphering Cryptic Messages
During the Great Depression of the 1930s, many people became homeless. Some of them traveled the country in search of work. They were called hobos. They sometimes would approach homes where they might ask for food or a place to sleep for the night. To help their fellow hobos, they would leave chalk or charcoal signs on fences or curbs – in a code so that the residents might not notice and remove them. There were a lot of signs, and some looked like this:

Hobo signs

The hobos who understood the signs had the advantage of knowing what behaviors to expect when they visited these homes or farms.

Like many other hardware manufacturers, Avid uses similar codes, but instead of chalk marks, they use LEDs and colors to convey some of the states of the surface.

Reading Spill Zone LED Signals
Avid's documentation describes the LEDs of "active" spill lights as being white, when most humans would describe them as bright blue. I will use "white" just to be compliant, but they look bright blue to me.

It is easy to spill and unspill tracks into Spill Zones, and easy to lose track of what is spilled where. When mixing, you will be better able to understand and control the current state of the console if you can quickly read the signals on those **L Spill**, **R Spill**, **Nudge** and **Bank** buttons.

Spill Button LED Rules

Each Spill Zone will be in one of three states indicated by the LED on the **L Spill** or **R Spill** button on the Master Module.

"Spill" LED State	Meaning
Unlit	The Spill Zone is not enabled (empty).
White (Bright Blue)	Spill zone is active. Spilling actions will spill into this zone and **B&N** buttons will act on this Spill Zone.
Colored	Tracks are spilled into this Spill Zone. The color indicates the element that is spilled.

Bank and Nudge Button LED Rules

Each button will be in one of four states.

"B&N" LED State	Meaning
Unlit	No tracks are available to bank.
Lit any color	Tracks are available to bank in the direction of lit button(s).
White (bright blue)	**B&N** buttons will perform normal banking.
Colored	**B&N** buttons will bank the activated Spill Zone (white Spill LED).
	The **B&N** LED color indicates element type that will be banked.

Element Colors

Element Type	L Spill/R Spill LED	Channel Strip Menu LED
VCA Master	Dark Green	Dark Green
VCA GM	Dark Green	Light Green
Layouts	Dark Blue	Dark Blue
Track Type	Pink	Pink
Workstation	Light Blue	Light Blue

Spill Zone Examples

The unlit **Spill** buttons indicate that nothing is spilled into either Spill Zone.

Nothing spilled

The white (bright blue) LEDs on all **B&N** buttons indicate that there are un-displayed tracks off to the right *and* the left – which can be banked to the surface using those buttons.

The **B&N** buttons will bank normally because nothing is spilled to a Spill Zone.

The Dark Blue **L Spill** LED indicates that a Layout is spilled to the Left Spill Zone. It is enabled, but not active, so the Left Spill Zone will not be banked by the **B&N** buttons.

Layout spilled

The white (bright blue) LEDs on the right **B&N** buttons indicate that there are un-displayed tracks off to the right – which can be banked normally.

Because elements are spilled into the Left Spill Zone, the **B&N** buttons will only bank into tracks which are not in the Left Spill Zone.

The Dark Green **R Spill** LED indicates that a VCA master is spilled to the Right Spill Zone.

VCA Master spilled within the Spill Zone

The white (bright blue) LED on the **L Spill** button indicates that the Left Spill Zone is active. Any spilling actions will spill into the Left Spill Zone.

The Left Spill Zone has not had any elements spilled into it. The **B&N** buttons will not bank anything, since they are not lit.

The Dark Green **R Spill** LED indicates that a VCA master is spilled to the Right Spill Zone.

VCA Master spilled beyond the Spill Zone

The white (bright blue) LED on the **L Spill** button indicates that the Left Spill Zone is active. Any spilling actions will spill into the Left Spill Zone.

The Dark Blue **B&N** buttons indicate that a Layout is spilled into the active Left Spill Zone. The selected Track Layout is larger than the Spill Zone, so **B&N** buttons will bank that Layout within that Spill Zone.

Chapter 13
Track Layouts and the Tracks Screen

Searching, banking, and scrolling through tracks to find the ones you need during a mix are non-creative tasks which can devour the time and energy you have for mixing. Wouldn't it be great if you could press one button to place all source music tracks in front of you, or all BGs or all submasters? This could significantly diminish the amount of time spent searching, and keep you focused on the creative aspects of your job. Track Layouts offer this capability.

To understand how best to use Track Layouts you must understand the functioning of the Tracks Screen – where Track Layouts are managed.

What are Track Layouts?
Track Layouts are a sets of surface maps (configurations) which, when recalled, place the mapped collection of tracks onto the surface in place of banking-mode layout.

Track Layouts give the user another way to assign tracks to channel strips, Master Meter modules, Master Post modules, and Joystick modules. Users can create, name, edit, save, and recall Track Layouts.

Track Layout Rules
- Tracks can be placed in any order within a Layout.
- Tracks may be placed multiple times within a single Layout.
- Tracks from different workstations, even different applications, may be intermingled within a Track Layout.
- A Track Layout may take up the entire surface, or only a few channel strips.
- A Track Layout will always occupy the same number of channel strips, regardless of how many tracks are included in the Track Layout.

DOI: 10.4324/9781003111801–16

- A Track Layout may be assigned to a Spill Zone or to the unspilled surface.
- Track Layouts are saved as sets. Track Layout sets are saved or loaded from files, either Title files or Pro Tools sessions, depending on User Preferences.
- A Layout Set can contain 1 to 98 Track Layouts, but if you find yourself making more than 12, you are probably over-doing it (*see "User Preferences" on page 32*).
- The default number of tracks in a Track Layout is the number of physical tracks of the system, but it can be changed using the Local Options (✿) of the Tracks Screen.
- Individual Track Layouts cannot be exported to or imported from another set, and a workstation application session or Title File can save or contain only one set at a time.

Whew! That's a lot of rules.

Layouts can enhance the use of VCA spilling, or they can work without VCA spilling, as you will see.

What Is the Difference Between Track Layouts and Spill Zones?

Spill Zones define where on the console spilling might take place, while Track Layouts define which tracks will be displayed on the surface, and their sequence.

Different from Spill zones, active Track Layouts occupy the surface channel strips, even if no track is assigned to a strip within the layout.

For example, if the S6 is set to Layout Mode but the session that is open does not contain the specific tracks that the current layout should display, the S6 will still reserve surface space for the Layout tracks, sometimes leaving the entire console empty of tracks, even though the DAW session contains tracks (*see "Searching the Bank" on page 205*).

Another significant way in which Layout Mode differs from spilling is in dealing with multiple workstations. The S6 can connect simultaneously to multiple workstations (i.e., multiple computers running Pro Tools, or one computer running Pro Tools, another running Logic Pro, and another running Audition). It is possible to create layouts which contain tracks from multiple workstations. Tracks 1–8 could be sourced from Pro Tools and tracks 9–16 could be sourced from Logic Pro, and so on.

One advantage of working with Track Layouts is that you can instantly popu-late the surface with a customized, predictable set of tracks. The S6, however, allows you to create layouts which contain more tracks than the surface can hold, necessitating banking to find the tracks you seek. I recommend that you limit Track Layouts to the surface space that you have.

Two Other Great Features of Track Layouts

- Tracks retain their display format (Display Layout) when the Track Layout is recalled.
- Joystick assignments which are assigned when the Track Layout is created can be recalled when the Track Layout is recalled.

Cut to the Chase – Track Layouts

1. Create, name, store, and save one or more Track Layouts.
2. Press **Layout Mode** on the Lower Master Module Locations section.
3. On the Master Module Soft Key pad, select a desired Track Layout.

Track Layouts can also be selected from the Layout Grid of the Tracks Screen.

Step #1 is the time-consuming step; the others are a breeze to use.

To return to Banking Mode (de-activate Layout Mode):

- Press **mmShift + Layout Mode**.

De-selecting a Track Layout returns the normal (Banking Mode) configuration of the surface. More details on this will follow, after you have created a few layouts.

The Tracks Screen

The Tracks Screen on the Master Module Touchscreen is where Track Layouts are managed. As usual, some background knowledge will make it easier for users to master Track Layouts, and you will learn a lot more about Tracks Screen along the way.

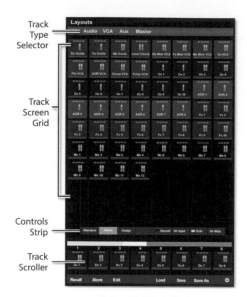

Track Type Selector

Track Screen Grid

Controls Strip

Track Scroller

Areas of the Tracks Screen

The Parts of the Tracks Screen

There are a lot of parts, so pay attention!

To reach the Tracks Screen, do one of these:

- On the Touchscreen, navigate to **Home > Tracks**.
- On the Master Module press **Tracks** button.

The Tracks Grid

Across the top 2/3 of the Track Screen is a grid (or matrix) with a block icon representing each track in the session.

The grid may be scrolled to reveal additional tracks or track types.

Filtering and Navigating the Track Grid

Above the grid is a strip of Track Type selectors, which select either All tracks, or filter the display to show only one type, such as audio tracks or Aux tracks.

To filter the type of track displayed, do one of these:

- Touch a Track Type selector.
- Swipe until you encounter the desired type.
- Touch or swipe to All to display unfiltered tracks.

To view the next page within a Track Type:

- Swipe down.

Swipe right, beyond the tracks in your session, and filtered windows will display, just as if you had touched a Track Type selector above. The Track Type selectors will light to indicate the current filter type. Swipe left or touch **All** to return to the unfiltered Track Grid.

Swipe All Day Long

If you continue swiping either direction, the selection of tracks cycles back to All, and continues for as long as you continue swiping.

Color Breaks

The display can be configured to start a new row of track icons every time the track color changes. This is most valuable when the tracks in the Pro Tools Session are colored with that intent.

Set this option in the Local Options (✿) setting window of the Tracks Screen.

Set Local Options

Controls Strip

Below the Track Grid is a strip of controls. They are contextual; they will change depending on what else you are doing in the Tracks Screen.

Controls Strip actions will be explored as we work through the Tracks Screen features.

Scrollers

Across the bottom of the Tracks Screen is a Universe View strip, and the Track Scroller, both of which match those on the Home screen. When the **Assign** Mode is invoked in the Controls Strip, the Track Scroller becomes the Strip Scroller, as described below. The Tracks Scroller has some local option settings which you might want to explore (*see Track Selector options on page 221*).

What You Can Do on the Tracks Screen

On the Tracks Screen, you may select tracks, attention tracks, set the RISM[1] mode of tracks, or build Track Layouts. There will be more details on these in the section "More Uses of the Tracks Screen" on page 146. Right now, we're looking at creating Layouts.

Using Layout Mode

Layout Mode may be invoked in several ways, with different results.

To enable Layout Mode, do one of these:

- Press the **Layout Mode** button on the Master module.
  - The first two pages of Layouts will occupy both Soft Key pads of the Master Module, but no Layout will be recalled to the surface.
  - The Layout pages may occupy these Soft Key pads until you press **Close** on one of them, depending on settings.

---

1. Record, Input, Solo, or Mute.

- Press **mmShift + Layout Mode** button.
  - The last-selected Layout will be recalled to the surface.
  - Press **Layout Mode** again to display Track Layouts on the Soft Key pad.
- Touch **Recall** on the Tracks Screen.
- Touch a Layout on the Touchscreen matrix.
- Touch **Load** on the Tracks Screen and load a saved Layout Set on the matrix.

If no Track Layouts have been created, or if the currently-loaded layout tracks are not open in a workstation, the assigned layout channel strips will be empty of tracks.

To enable Layout Mode, ready to Assign tracks:

- Touch **Assign** on the Tracks Screen.
  The LED on the **Layout Mode** button will light white when Layout Mode is active.

To exit Layout Mode, do one of these:

  - Press **mmShift + Layout Mode** button.
  - If a Layout is active, press the Soft Key of that Layout.

Layout Sets and the Layout Grid

Collections of Track Layouts are called Layout Sets. They may be created, saved, and recalled using the menu at the bottom of the Tracks Screen. Only one Layout Set can be active at one time. The contents of a Layout Set may be viewed, edited, or stored via the Layout Grid.

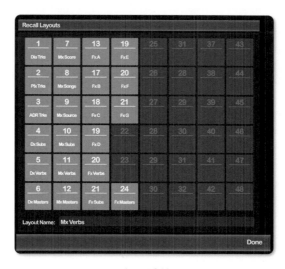

Layout Grid

The Layout Grid is a matrix which presents all individual Layouts that are in the active Layout Set. The location of each Layout in the grid represents where each Layout will appear on Soft Key pads. The six boxes in the first column of the grid are assigned to the Soft Keys on the left side of the first Soft Key page, the second column is the right side, the third and fourth columns will be assigned to the second Soft Key page, and so on.

Tasks that you can perform from the Layout Grid depend on how the grid is reached.

Button Used	Location of Button	Task
Assign	Control Strip	Create, name, edit the contents of Layouts.
Edit	Touchscreen Lower Soft Keys	Edit the locations or names of Layouts in the Grid. Delete Layouts. The contents of Layouts cannot be edited here, only names and grid positions.
Recall	Touchscreen Lower Soft Keys	Recall Layouts to the surface.
Store	Touchscreen Lower Soft Keys	Only available when Assign is enabled. Name and Store Layouts into their grid positions.

A slightly confusing thing is that "Edit" is where you edit the Layout Set itself, not the Track Layouts which are contained within the Layout Set. Here, you can change the name and position of a Layout within in the Layout Grid. The contents are changed in Assign Mode.

Preparing to Create Layouts

There are a few things to do before actually creating Track Layouts: setting the layout width and clearing layouts.

Layout Width

Unlike spilling, Layouts will try to occupy their full width regardless of how many tracks are assigned to them. If you have five tracks in a 24-track wide Layout, there will be 19 empty channel strips on the surface. Depending on your needs, it may be advisable to adjust the width.

By default, the S6 creates Layouts that are the width of the surface hardware. That width may be adjusted to 8–256 strips.

When that value exceeds the available number of physical strips, banking works on the Layout strips. Avid refers to this as Virtual Strips, although it behaves no differently than Banking Mode.

To set Layout Width:

1. On the Touchscreen, navigate to the Local Options (✿) of the Tracks Screen.
2. Adjust the slider.

Clearing Unwanted Layouts

You should presume that the system on which you are working is already cluttered with leftover and unwanted Layouts. Let's be sure they're clear before we clutter it up with our own Layouts.[2]

To clear all Layouts:

1. On the Touchscreen, navigate to **Tracks > Edit** to display the Layout Grid.
2. Touch `Delete All.`
3. Touch `Delete` to confirm.

Creating Track Layouts

Cut to the Chase: Creating a Track Layout:

1. Enter Layout Assign Mode.
2. Assemble tracks from the Tracks grid into the Strip Scroller in the sequence and position where you want them displayed on the S6 surface.
3. Store the Layout into the active Layout Set, giving that Layout a name, and placing it into a position in the Layout Grid, where it will eventually appear in Layout pages of the Soft Key pads.
4. When a Layout Set is complete, save that Layout Set to a file or to a DAW session, depending on user preferences. If you store a Layout but do not save the Layout Set, the Layout will be lost after a restart.

To Enter Layout Assign Mode:

- On the Tracks Screen, touch `Assign`.

Tracks Screen – Layout Assign

---

2. If you loaded the Title and Preference files available with this book, there should be no Layout clutter.

This looks nearly identical to the Attention or Select mode except that **Assign** is lit, **Insert Strip**, **Delete Strip,** and **Clear Strip** appear on the Controls Strip, and a set of management commands appears across the lower Soft Keys.

If **Insert Strip**, **Delete Strip,** and **Clear Strip** do not appear on the control strip, check so see if **L Spill** or **R Spill** are lit. If so, turn them off.

The Track Scroller has changed to the Strip Scroller, which looks identical to the Tracks Scroller, so you will have to exercise some trust in the system.

The Strip Scroller Explained

Consider the Strip Scroller to be the working area where you will assemble the list of tracks which will become a named Track Layout. After you have assigned the tracks in their desired sequence in the Strip Scroller, you store its contents into an individual Track Layout, placing it into the Layout Set Grid. You must then save the Layout Set to a file.

Each slot block in the Strip Scroller is a "strip" which represents a channel strip on the surface. The strips are numbered, counting from the left of the surface. You will place (assign) track blocks from the Track Grid into the strips in the Strip Scroller. While in Assign Mode, the surface will reflect the track assignments in the Strip Scroller, which makes it easy to confirm your strip placements by looking at the surface.

When Layout Assignment mode is entered, the last-recalled Layout will be loaded into the Strip Scroller. You may edit that configuration and save it, or you may want to clear it out and start from scratch.

To clear (empty) the Strip Scroller (and start building a Layout from scratch):

1. Hold **mmShift**.
   The **Clear Strip** command becomes **Clear All**.
2. Touch **Clear All.**

When adding or removing tracks in the Strip Scroller, their behaviors are controlled by the **Insert**, **Delete Strip,** and **Clear Strip** commands in the Controls Strip. Keep in mind that "Strip" refers to individual channel strip(s), not the horizontal row of channel strips.

Insert switches between overwriting or shuffling when a strip is added. When **Insert** is lit, added strips will push existing strips to the right to make room. When it is not lit, added strips will overwrite existing strips.

Delete Strip removes the strip, allowing existing strips to slide to the left to take up empty slots.

Clear Strip clears the strip from the strip slot, leaving it empty in place.

Selecting Tracks in the Track Grid
To select tracks:
- Touch a track to select. Touch a selected track to de-select.
- Touch and hold a track, then swipe across additional tracks to select contiguous tracks.
- Touch and hold a track. While holding it, touch other tracks to select or de-select them.

To add Tracks to the Strip Scroller:
1. Confirm that **Delete Strip** and **Clear Strip** are not active, and that **Insert** is lit (shuffling) or unlit (overwriting).

Insert: Add Tracks – Shuffling

2. Scroll the Strip Scroller to display the track slot where you want to assign the selected track(s).
3. Select one or more tracks in the Track Grid.
   Select them in the sequence that you want them added into the Layout.
4. Touch the first destination block of the Strip Scroller.
   The selected tracks will be assigned to consecutive positions in the Strip Scroller and will display on the surface.
   Any unassigned strips will remain empty on the surface.
5. Repeat 2–4 until you are satisfied with the assembly.

To remove Tracks from the Strip Scroller:
Despite the words **Delete** and **Clear**, this process does not delete tracks. It removes tracks from the Strip Scroller only.
1. Scroll the Strip Scroller to display the track(s) you want to remove.
2. Set the removal behavior:
   - To leave an empty block, other tracks remain in same positions. Touch **Clear Strip**.
   - To shuffle other tracks to the left, filling the void, touch **Delete Strip.**

Clear Strip: remove tracks – leaving them empty   Remove Tracks – shuffling

3. Touch a track in the Strip Scroller. It will be removed.

Delete Strip or **Clear Strip** mode will remain active until changed by the user.

The track assignments in the Strip Scroller must be stored into the Layout matrix for it to become part of the current Layout Set. *Afterwards, the Layout Set needs to be saved. That is another step.*

To Store the Strip Scroller as a Track Layout in the Current Layout Set:

1. Touch **Store** to open the Layout Grid. Store is only available through the Layout Assign Mode.
2. Touch a block in the Layout Grid, and a Layout Name field will appear.
3. Double-touch in the Layout Name field and give the Layout a name.
   If you do not enter a name the system will give it a number, but it is best to give each Layout a name which describes what it is.
4. Press **Store** again, and this Layout will become part of the current Layout Set. This is an easy step to forget. If you do not store the Layout, it will not become part of the set.

FYI – The same procedure for assigning tracks to Track Layouts is used when assigning tracks to the Master Post Module and the Master Joystick Module.

To create a Track Layout based on the currently-banked tracks:

1. From the Tracks page, touch the local settings icon (small gear bottom right corner) and confirm that **Double Tap Assign to Copy Tracks from Banking Mode into Current Layout** is selected.
2. In the workstation, arrange the tracks into the sequence you want the Layout to become. Use Hide for unwanted tracks.

3. Double-touch the `Assign` button on the Tracks Screen, and a layout arrangement will be created in the Strip Scroller.
4. Press `Store`, then place and name that Layout.
5. Save the Layout Set when finished.

Creating a Track Layout based on the currently-banked tracks is only helpful if the tracks have already been assembled and banked, otherwise it is much easier to build the Layout in the Strip Scroller. Building Layouts based on currently-banked tracks limits the tracks to one workstation. *If Double Tap Assign to Copy Tracks from Banking Mode in Current Layout is left on, the feature could be confusing at a later time.*

Saving or Loading the Layout Set

When creating, deleting, or editing is complete you must save the Layout Set, either to a Title File or to the Pro Tools Session. If you do not, it may vanish.

To Save Layout Set to the designated workstation application (i.e., Pro Tools):

- Confirm that the S6 is configured to save Titles and Preferences to the designated application's session file.
- Double-press **Save** on the Master Module. Its LED should blink and then go dark. The current Layout Set is saved within the workstation session. (Pressing **Command + S** on the Pro Tools keyboard will do the same thing.)

To manually save a Layout Set to a Title File:

1. On the Touchscreen, navigate to the **Layouts Assign** screen.
2. Touch **Save** or **Save As** in the Assign Tracks Screen.
3. Navigate to the location to which you want to save the Title File.
4. Double-touch in the Title File Name field and type in a Title File name,
5. Touch **Save**.

To load a Layout Set from a Title File:

1. From the bottom of the Tracks Screen touch **Load**.
2. Navigate to the Title File.
3. Touch **Open**.

Recalling Track Layouts

After creating a few layouts, forget about the Touchscreen for a minute and check out how easily this can work during a mix.

To recall a Track Layout (easy):
- Be sure that no Spill Zones are active.
  - If they are, press **mmShift +** the lit Spill Zone button.
- On the Master Module press **Layout Mode** or **mmShift + Layout Mode**.
  - Using **mmShift** will recall the last-used Layout to the surface.
- On the Softkey Layout page, press any Layout selection, and it will be recalled to the surface.
- Press **mmShift + Layout Mode** and the surface will return to Banking Mode.

To recall a Track Layout (not-as-easy):
- From Tracks Screen, touch **Recall**, and a Layout Grid will display.
- Touch the desired Layout Name on the grid, and it will be recalled.

To recall a Track Layout to a Spill Zone:
- Press **L Spill** or **R Spill**, then recall a Track Layout (*see above*).

The Layout will spill into the chosen Spill Zone.

Although it took a few minutes to create the Track Layouts, they are amazing tools for navigating through a big session quickly and reliably. Layouts are easy to edit. I think they're fun.

Editing Track Layouts

Maybe you flawlessly designed and created the Track Layout(s) exactly as you wish, and you will never change your mind. But sometimes you need to do some adjusting.

To edit the location, name or existence – but not the contents – of a Track Layouts:
1. Enable Layout Mode (*see page 138*).
2. Navigate to **Tracks > Edit** on the Touchscreen.

To move an individual Layout to a different position in the matrix:
1. Touch and hold its box until the box ghosts.
2. Drag it to a different grid block.

To rename a Layout:
1. Touch the Layout's box.
2. Edit the name in the Layout Name field.
3. Touch **Done**.

To delete an individual Layout:
1. Touch and hold its box until the box ghosts.
2. Drag it off the grid.

To delete all individual Layouts:
1. Touch **Delete All**.
2. Touch **Delete** to confirm.

To Edit the contents of a Layout:
Do it the same way you created it.
1. Navigate to **Tracks** Screen and enter **Layout Mode** (*see page 138*).
2. Select the Individual Layout which you want to edit. Its track strips will populate the Track Scroller.
3. Touch **Assign**, then add, remove, or move strips in the Strip Scroller.
4. Press **Store** when editing is complete. The Layout Grid will open.
5. Touch the Layout block to which you want to save the edited Layout – probably the one you selected in step 2.
6. Touch **Store** once again to save that change.

Do not forget to save the Layout Set (*See "Saving or loading the Layout Set" on page 144*).

More Uses of the Tracks Screen
There are even more things which may be done on the Tracks Screen. Many of these actions can be accomplished easily or quickly on the surface or in the Pro Tools screen. If it is not convenient to use the mouse and keyboard the Touchscreen gives you some options.

To Attention a Track from the Tracks Screen Grid:
1. Touch **Attention** to engage Attention mode.
2. Touch a track in the Track Grid, and it will be assigned to the Attention Track Editor and the Attention Track Fader.

Attention
Mode

Set Attention Mode

To select Tracks from the Tracks Screen Grid:

1. Touch **Select** to engage Select mode.
2. Touch a track or tracks in the Track Grid to select it.
   o Selection is additive.
3. Touch a selected track to de-select it.
4. To select multiple contiguous tracks, touch and hold the first track for about a second, then drag across any other tracks you wish to select.

Select
Mode

Set Select Mode

To set RISM from the Tracks Screen Grid:

1. Touch **Record** or **Input** or **Solo** or **Mute** to engage this mode.
2. Touch a track in the Track Grid and the selected setting will be applied to that track.
3. Solo will behave in inter-cancel or switch mode, depending on user settings.
4. Touch **Attention**, **Select,** or **Assign** to deactivate this mode.

Set R I S M

Part IV
Options and Extras

In the first three parts, we explored the basic and intermediate features of the S6 which are available to most users and which give high levels of power and flexibility. Most of us can turn these features into solid action when mixing a project.

But that's not all, folks. There are still more modules and features and techniques to explore. If they interest you, they are great tools for your tool box.

Chapter 14

Master Meter Modules

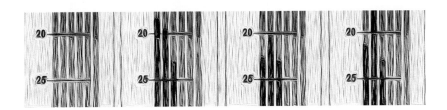

As I said somewhere else in this book, the basic S6 does not have dedicated meters. The good news, though, is that dedicated meters can be created, and those meters are quite good meters. The bad news is that they take up some resources. They must occupy a Display Module. That Display Module may be one of the standard "Top of the Channel Strip" modules or it could be an additional Display Module installed exclusively for this purpose.

Introducing the Master Meter Modules

Any Display Module can be designated as a dedicated meter display called a Master Meter Module. If the Display Module is a part of a channel strip chassis, that designation disconnects the Display Module from the tracks below. Because of this, using Master Meter Modules is more effective when the Display Module is not installed as a part of a channel strip. But sometimes it is necessary or desirable to hijack a Display Module (or two) for this purpose.

The Master Meter Module displays eight columns of meters, in one to four rows. The more rows displayed, the shorter each meter is, and in my opinion, the less helpful it is.

Three meter types are available: **Large Meters**, **Large Waveforms**, and **Meters and Waveforms**.

DOI: 10.4324/9781003111801-18

Large Meters

Large Waveforms

Meters and Waveforms

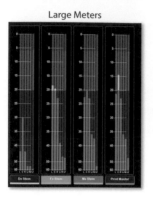
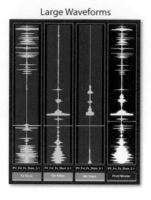
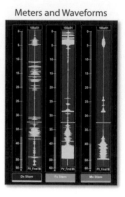

Master Meter types

Meter Layouts assign the position and choice of tracks to be displayed. Many *Meter Layouts* may be created and stored, and recalled via the Soft Key pads. *Meter Layouts* may also be linked to Track Layouts so that the *Meter Layout* will be recalled automatically when a linked Track Layout is recalled.

Meter types can be changed using the Tracks screen Local Options (✿), using Soft Keys, or by pressing **mmShift + Display 1** or **mmShift + Display 2** on the Master Module while in Meters view.

Cut to the Chase: To Use a Master Meter Module

1. Designate a Display Module as a Master Meter Module in Meters View. This is the step that will get you into trouble with your studio engineers if you do it without their approval.
2. Determine the type of meters you want to show, and how many rows (1–4) you want to use and set those choices in the **Tracks > Local Options (✿)** screen.
3. Create, name, save, and store one or more Meter Layouts, linking them to Track Layouts as you go.

Designating a Display Module as Master Meter Module
Enter Meters View by doing one of these:

- Navigate to **Home > Meters** on the Touchscreen.
- Navigate to **Tracks > Meters** on the Touchscreen.

Here's how to build it.

To designate an existing Display Module as a Master Meter Module:

1. On the Touchscreen, navigate to **Settings** > **Surface** > **Config** > **Display**.
2. Follow the instructions on the screen.
3. Press **Done** when finished or **Cancel** to exit.

To set the type of meter and number of meter rows of the Master Meter Module:

- On the Touchscreen, navigate to **Tracks** > **Local Options (✿)** > **Meter Layouts**
  - ○ Chose the **Layout Type** from the pull-down menu.
  - ○ Chose the **Number of Meter Rows** with the slider.

Creating Master Meter Layouts

To create Meter Layouts:

1. On the Home screen, touch **Meters**, or press **mmShift + Tracks** on the Master Module.
   This recalls the Meters Screen, which looks much like the Tracks Screen.
2. Touch **Assign** on the Meters Screen.
3. Select track(s) in the track matrix.
4. Touch a strip block in the lower matrix to assign selected track(s) to the desired position.
5. Repeat 3–4 until satisfied with the arrangement.
6. Touch **Store** and the **Store Meter Layouts** grid will appear.
7. Touch a block in the Store Meter Layouts grid to assign the current Meter Layout to a block.
8. To link this Meter Layout to an existing Track Layout, touch the desired Track Layout in the Store grid. The Meter Layout's number will be added to the Track Layout block.
9. You do not *have* to do this, but you should type a name into the Name field.
10. Touch **Store**.

As always, be aware that if you do not save the Meter Layouts to a Title file (or configured workstation application session), all this setup will be lost the next time a different Title File or designated workstation session is loaded or opened on the S6.

To adjust the Waveform zoom size in all meters, do one of these:

- On the Touchscreen, navigate to **Settings** > **User** > **Master Meter Display** and adjust **Waveform Zoom**.
- After a Master Meter Module has been assigned:
  - ○ On Touchscreen, navigate to Home > Meters.
  - ○ Press **mmShift + Display 1** or **mmShift + Display 2** on the Master Module to cycle through display choices.

Show Automation, Reverse Automation Lanes, and Automation Opacity settings are universal across all of the S6's Display Modules. They are adjusted in **Settings** > **User** > **Display Module**.

Un-Designating a Master Meter Module

To deactivate a Master Meter Module, relinquishing it back to the track's module:

1. On the Touchscreen, navigate to **Settings** > **Surface** > **Config** > **Display**.
2. Touch `clear`.
3. Touch **Done**.

Chapter 15

The Master Post Module

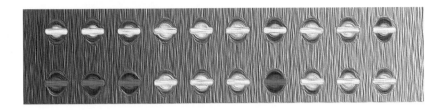

Some S6 systems are supercharged for cinema mixing and re-recording – especially aimed at the Old-School Mixer. If you are so lucky to have the Master Post Module or the Master Joystick Module (next chapter) installed on your S6, it is time to learn how to use them!

Introducing the Master Post Module

The Master Post Module (MPM) provides mixers with a traditional cinema recorder control surface. From here recorder tracks can be soloed and muted, armed or dis-armed for recording, or made safe from accidental recording.

The MPM also offers its own set of Monitoring Buttons to control speaker selection and monitoring types, mirroring the same controls of the Monitoring Screen of the Touchscreen. These buttons can be customized using the standard Soft Key editor of the S6, giving mixers fixed buttons to control their choice of features.

The Post Module

DOI: 10.4324/9781003111801-19

An additional Soft Key pad on this module gives mixers access to specific Soft Key pages where Post Layouts can be recalled, as well as the ability to add custom Soft Key pages.

More than one Post Module can be installed to accommodate multiple mixers. Multiple MPMs can be configured to work independently or mirror one-another.

A row of what look like modifier keys below the strips only indicate the color of the assigned track, if any. They have no other function.

Why use the Master Post Module?
The Mixing Process (A Little Background)

No movie is mixed, printed, and delivered. It is mixed, reviewed, changed, reviewed, changed, shown to director, changed, shown to director and producer, changed, taken to a theater and previewed to a recruited audience. Repeat as many of these steps as the budget allows. Eventually, when time, money, patience, and crew are exhausted, the mix is deemed to be finished.

During this process the reviewers expect to see a complete and flawless playback of the work that has been done, and there is hell to pay if, during Playback, the mix chokes, sputters or stops.

The Mixer

The mixer is responsible for creating a virtual mix of the project. This mix could reside within one workstation session or may be spread across multiple workstation sessions. In this form, the mix may not be very portable, since it requires the same number and configuration of workstations and playback systems whenever it is played. Even when played back in the venue in which it is created, a virtual mix is vulnerable to a hiccup or failure of any system, and on very complex mixes, this could mean a high risk of failure.

Deliverable Elements

As well as a creative mix, the mixer must also create the deliverable elements: actual recorded flat[1] files in a variety of formats, specified in the production contracts. These might include:

- Dialog Only Stem   5.1 (or other theatrical format).
- Effects Only Stem   5.1 (or other theatrical format).
- Music Only Stem   5.1 (or other theatrical format).

---

1. Complete, uninterrupted files running from start to finish.

- Print Master 5.1 (or other theatrical format).
- Dialog, effects, and music fold-downs (mono, stereo, Lt/Rt or other formats).
- Print Master fold-downs (mono, stereo, Lt/Rt, or other formats).
- Many other variations possible.

Finding a Solution

Because we seek a way to make a mix portable and diminish the risk of failure during playbacks, and because we must create these deliverable elements at some point in the project, we incorporate the creation of stems and print masters within our mixing workflow. While this adds a bit of time to the mix process, it gives us some advantages as well.

- Creating a recorded print master allows playback of the mix in any professional screening room.
- Creating recorded stems allows elements for each stem to be taken off-line without disrupting the mixing of other stem elements.
- Changes being made to one element need only be punched (recorded) into one stem and the print master.
- Copies or crash-downs of recorded stems can be given to editorial for QC and other purposes.

The common workflow for cinema mixes:

- Mix a first or second virtual pass through a reel, act, or section.
  Play back that pass for review, recording stems and print master simultaneously. This gives us a "protection" copy at the very least.
- Subsequently, as mix changes are made, punch (record) them into any affected stem and print master.

This process requires much punching in and out on the recorder and much comparing of already-recorded audio (playback) with virtual-playing audio (input). That is where this master module becomes a very useful tool.

Using the paddles and other record-track controls is easy. Configuring the controls is more complicated, but very much like configuring Track Layouts. Let's look at how the controls should be used, then see how to configure them.

Using Post Layouts for the Master Post Module

None of the Post Module's features will give you much utility until you make assignments of tracks to the strips of the MPM. This is done by creating Post Layouts. Like other S6 Layout types, Post Layouts can be created, saved, and recalled when needed.

Before creating Post Layouts, navigate to **Tracks > Local Options (✿)> Number of Post Strips in Post Layout** and adjust the setting to the number of tracks you would like to make available. The possible range is 10 to 80. If you assign more than ten on a single MPM, you will need to bank the tracks to strips to access them all.

Creating Post Layouts

Post Layouts are created from the Tracks Screen while in Assign Post mode, which is only available when a Post Module is installed.

To enter Assign Post mode:

1. On the Touchscreen, navigate to the **Tracks** screen.
2. Press and hold **mmShift**.
   The **Assign** button becomes **Assign Post**.
3. Touch **Assign Post**.

Tracks Screen – enter Assign Post mode

The strip scroller at the bottom of the Tracks Screen becomes the Post strip scroller, each block now representing a strip slot on the MPM.

To assign tracks to the Post strips:

1. Focus the desired application or workstation to the Tracks Matrix.
2. Select a track or block of tracks from the Tracks Grid.
3. Touch the strip block in the post scoller, starting where you want the selection assigned.
4. Repeat 1–3 until all desired tracks have been placed.
5. When all tracks are placed, touch **Store**.
   The **Store Post Layouts** grid will appear. Placed tracks in the strip stroller will be outlined in green. If they are not green, they will not be included in the Post Layout.

Post scroller

6. Touch any strip blocks in the strip scroller to include or exclude them, indicated by the green outline.
7. Touch a block in the Layouts Grid to assign this Layout a position and number.
   The Layout Name field will appear as well as a **Store** button.
8. Enter a name for this Post Layout then touch **Enter** in the dialog box.
   The Post Layout will be stored into the grid with its name and the grid number.
   You do not have to enter a name, but you should!
9. If you do not want to enter a name, touch the new **Store** button and the Post Layout will be stored with only a number to identify it.
10. Touch **Assign Post** to exit Assign Post mode.

Post Layouts will be stored in the Title memory, where they will remain volatile but active. They can be lost by a system crash, restart, or possibly by loading a new Pro Tools session. Post layouts should be saved, either by saving the Title File (*see "To manually save or load a Title to or from a file" on page 36*) or, if configured to do so, with the workstation session (*see "Designate Pro Tools Sessions for automatic preference use" on page 37*). The best option is to do both.

Recalling Post Layouts

Post Layouts may be recalled from the Touchscreen, from the Master Module Softkey pads, or from the MPM Softkey pad.

To recall Post Layouts from the Touchscreen:

1. On the Touchscreen, navigate to the Tracks Screen.
2. While holding **mmShift** touch **Assign Post**.
3. Touch **Recall**.
   The recall grid will open.
4. Touch the desired Layout in the Layout Grid.
5. Tap **Done** to close the grid.

To recall Post Layouts from a Master Module Softkey pad:

1. On the Touchscreen, navigate to the Tracks Screen.
2. Press **Layout Mode** button on the Lower Master Module.
3. While holding **mmShift** touch **Assign Post** on the Tracks Screen.
   Assign Post should light purple.
4. On the Soft Key pad of the Master Module select the desired Post Layout.
5. Press **Close** in the navigation section of Soft Key pad to release the pad.

Using the Master Post Module Track Record Controls

Switches (paddles) on the upper row set the record status of the assigned tracks to Record On or Record Off.

When a strip is recording, the recorder paddle lights red. When not recording, the recorder paddle lights blue or off, depending on user settings and record mode.[2] With this setting turned on, record paddles will light blue if Track Punch or Destructive Punch are activated. They will not light in other record modes.

Post Module paddle switches

Switches (paddles) on the lower row switch the assigned tracks to Input or Playback mode. The paddle of a track lights green when it is set to Playback.

Because the paddles are not toggle buttons, the mixer does not need to know their current status before pressing them. Regardless of the paddle's beginning setting, pushing the lower paddle down always switches to Playback. Up always switches to Input. On the upper row, up sets Record On, down sets Record Off.

When recording, you want RECORD on, and the monitor set to Input. Push both paddles upward.

When playing back, you want RECORD off and the monitor set to Playback. Push both paddles downward.

When rehearsing, you want RECORD off, and the monitor set to Input so that you can hear any adjustments you are making to the mix. Record paddle down, monitor paddle up.

Sometimes when rehearsing, we want to compare our current virtual mix to the recorded mix. Flipping the monitor paddle up and down gives us an easy way to switch between input and playback, comparing the two states.

Mixing in the Green

A mistake that is easy to make after an initial record pass is to rehearse mix changes while listening to Playback. Mix changes take place in the tracks but are not heard in the studio. This is called "Mixing in the Green." If you find yourself making mix changes that you do not hear, this is the first thing to check.

The best way to avoid mixing in the green is to get into the habit of always pushing both the record and monitoring paddles down when punching out of record. You will still get caught from time to time.

---

2. See User > Surface > Strips / Use Pro Tools Tracks Record Mode Colors.

The MPM offers three essential controls for each record track: Solo, Mute, and Ready (SMR). Solo and mute are easy to understand. Ready arms the track for record. If Ready is not lit red, the track will not go into record.

Linking Strips
Not Enough Fingers

Sometimes the mixer needs to work several or all ten paddles of the MTM at the same time. At most, mixers have four fingers and maybe a thumb on each hand, which is not enough digits to work more than five tracks at a time with one hand. There are four options to give just one paddle the power to rule them all, which requires only one digit:

- Basic Link   Any linked strip controls all linked strips.
- Link Master   A Master strip controls all linked strips.
                              Individual strips can be controlled independently.
- Ready buttons   Restrains control of record punches.
- Master Record Master strip controls punch in only.

Using Basic Link

Basic Linking connects the controls of two or more tracks so that any action of the paddles and SMR buttons is applied to all linked tracks.

To link strips:

1. Press the Master Link button (upper-left corner).
   Its LED will flash yellow.
2. Press Link button of strips that you want linked.
   Their Link LED will flash yellow.
   Press Link button again if you need to de-select that strip from the link.
3. Bank to other strips if they are beyond reach. Link them.
4. When link selections are completed, press Master Link button again.
   Its LED will stop flashing but remain lit yellow.

Using Link Master

Link Master designates one strip as a Master. Paddles and SMR actions on the Master strips are applied to all linked strips, but actions taken on individual strips are independent of the Master or other linked strips.

This is a very common way to configure the MTM. All you need to do is designate that master, and other strips in the link will be controlled by that master.

Linking buttons

To designate a Link Master:
1. Press the **Attention** (△) and **Link Master** button (upper left of MPM) simultaneously.
   Both of their LEDs will flash yellow.
2. Press the **Link** button of the strip which you want to be the Link Master.
   The LEDs will stop flashing.
   Two horizontal lines will frame the name of the designated Link Master.

Using Ready Lights
This is a slightly sketchy way to control the punch in and out of multiple tracks, as it is more prone to making mistakes, but is a bit quicker for situations where your needs are quickly changing.

To use Ready buttons in Linked record mode:
1. Link all strips in which you might want to record, using either Basic Link or Link Master.
2. On any pass or sequence of passes, use the **Ready** buttons to arm only the strips which you want to record.
3. Dis-arm or arm strips as needed.
4. Punch in or out using either the Link Master or any Basic Linked strip.

Using Master Record
Yes, there is yet another option on the MPM called Master Record. In this mode, a designated strip will punch in all linked strips, but no other controls are linked. This gives you the power to punch in all linked strips with this Master Record track, punch out of the Master Record track without punching out of the other linked tracks.

To designate Master Record track:
1. Press the master Link button (upper left of module) for two seconds.
   All strip Link LEDs will flash quickly.

2. Press the flashing Link button on every strip you want to designate.
   The strip's Link button will stop flashing, remaining lit yellow.
   The name of the strip in its OLED will be framed by vertical lines.
3. When finished designating, press the master Link button again.

Banking Strips
Banking and Locking MPM strips

If you have assigned more than ten tracks to the current Post Layout, you must bank the MTM to bring additional tracks to the surface.

To bank strips:

- Press ◀ or ▶ on the MPM to bank strips left or right.

You may lock a track to the first strip on the MTM. This is especially handy if you are controlling more than ten tracks and are using a Link Master strip to control most of them. Lock that master to Strip 1 and you always have it showing.

To lock a track to Strip 1:

1. Adjust the Post Layout or bank tracks to place the desired track into Strip 1.
2. Press and hold Attention (△) button, then press the **Link** button of Strip 1.
   The name of the track in Strip 1 will be highlighted in yellow, indicating that it is locked.

But wait! There's more!

A valuable button hidden among the rarely-used Speaker Control buttons is Auto Match. This performs the same **Auto Match** function found on Automation Soft Key pages and on the Pro Tools Automation Window: it punch-glides out all automation parameters. Avid glued it right there where you can easily reach it. Before you punch out of record, it could be a good idea to hit **Auto Match** first.

Spilling Strips
VCA Spilling – An Alternative to Banking the Post Strips

The MPM allows the use of VCA Master spilling into the Post strips. Only one level of spilling is available.

You may assign record tracks to a VCA Master/group structure. Assign the VCA masters to Post strips. These masters may be spilled to reveal their GMs[3] on the paddles. When masters are displayed, the paddles pass record and monitor commands to their GMs. When GMs are displayed, their paddles control only the individual GM.

This is a very powerful tool, but it requires some pre-planning to make it work gracefully.

To spill a VCA Master within the MPM Post strips:

1. Set **Link Master** button to off (upper-left corner).
2. Recall a Post Layout containing one or more VCA Masters.
3. Bank the desired VCA Master into view on a Post strip.
4. Press the **Link** button of the VCA Master's Post strip.
   The VCA Master's GMs will spill into the Post strips.
   Use the banking (◄ or ►) buttons if necessary.
5. Press the **Link** button of any Post strip to un-spill the VCA Master.

---

3. GM = Group Member.

Chapter 16

The Joystick Module

Introducing the Joystick Module

The reasons for using this Master Module (MJM) are simple to understand. This optional module for the S6 adds some multi-channel panning capabilities to the surface. This is not an essential module; its advantages over panning done using the Function Editor on the Touchscreen are mostly ergonomic.

With the Master Joystick Module, it is much easier to operate the controls, as they are not on a nearly vertical surface. Having actual hardware to hold onto gives some mixers more fluidity in their work.

The display screen in the center depicts two surround fields and indicates the current pan position of the assigned tracks. In Pickup Mode, both the current pan position (underlying automation) and the current joystick position are displayed.

Like the Function Editor, the MJM allows the mixer to write two separate panning paths at the same time.

All fader section controls (except fader) of the two assigned tracks are available on the MJM.

The MJM features a "somewhat assignable" Knob Cluster for each of the two tracks. These Knob Clusters can be assigned to any pan parameters of their assigned channel.

The joysticks themselves may be configured to control any two parameters of the assigned track using the X (horizontal) and Y (vertical) axes. This feature, while cool sounding, is not likely to get much use.

A helpful feature of the MJM is that assignments of tracks can be saved and recalled along with Track Layouts.

DOI: 10.4324/9781003111801–20

From their position in front of the MJM a mixer has access to the useful controls. A batch of features to control the panning actions gives this module added value.

Joystick Module

Assigning Tracks to the Joystick Module

Before you can pan a track, it must be assigned to an MJM joystick. Assigning a track or tracks to the joystick controls seems simple, but there are a few tricks to keep assignments under control.

On S6 systems with an MJM installed, attentioning a track will assign it to the MJM, with some exceptions. Whether a track is assigned to the left or the right joystick is controlled by how those tracks are attentioned.

To assign a track to the left joystick:
- Attention the track by doing one of these:
  - Press the track's **Attention** (△) button.
  - On the Touchscreen's Tracks Screen touch **Attention**, then select a track in the Tracks Grid.

If the track has dual panners, such as a stereo track, the left panner is assigned to the left joystick, the right panner to the right joystick.

To assign two tracks to the two joysticks:
1. Attention the track for the left joystick.
2. Within two seconds,[1] attention the track for the right joystick.

---

1. The time allowed can be changed in Settings > User >Joystick Strips.

After two seconds, subsequent attentioning of a track will assign the new track to the left joystick.

Assigning incorrectly requires that you start over.

Locking Joystick Assignments

Once the desired assignments are made, you may want to lock them into place so that subsequent attentioning will not change them.

To lock a track to a joystick:

1. In the MJM track controls of the desired joystick section, hold **Attention** ($\triangle$).
2. A small **Lock** or **Unlock** image will appear in the OLED.
3. Press the button to the right of the **Menu** button, below the **Lock** or **Unlock** image.
4. When locked, a padlock will display in the joystick OLED.

To unlock a track from a joystick:

- In the MJM track controls of the desired joystick section, hold **Attention** ($\triangle$) and press **Menu**.

Assigning tracks to joysticks in Track Layouts.

In Layout Assign mode,[2] the Strip Scroller displays the joystick strips which, instead of strip numbers, are labeled **Joy1** and **Joy2** (in a violet bar). Tracks may be assigned to those joystick strips. The joystick assignments might be stored and recalled with that Track Layout. If the joystick strip is highlighted green when the Track Layout is stored, it will be stored (and saved) with the Track Layout. Before storing, you may toggle the green highlight by touching the joystick strip(s).

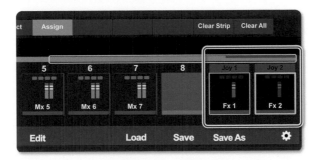

Joystick Strips in the Strip scroller

_____

2. See "Creating Track Layouts" on page 140.

> I cannot understand why Avid made highlighting necessary. Can't we just clear the strip if we do not want a joystick assigned by the layout?

The default state of the green highlighting can be set on or off in **Tracks > Local Options (✿) > Auto Select Joystick Strips when Storing Layouts**. Regardless of the default state, the highlighting can be toggled with a touch.

To assign track(s) to joystick(s) in a Track Layout:

1. Enter Layout Assign mode *(see page 140)*.
   (To add joystick assignment to an existing Track Layout, first recall the layout.)
2. Scroll the Strip Scroller to reveal **Joy 1** and **Joy 2**.
3. Touch desired track in the Tracks Grid, then touch the desired joystick strip.
4. Repeat #3 until desired choices are complete.
5. If necessary, touch joystick strips to toggle green highlighting. Highlighted strips will be saved with the Layout.
6. Touch **Store** and complete the store procedure.

Once a Track Layout is installed, the attentioning of any other track will overwrite the joystick assignment. I suggest you get into the habit of locking those joysticks.

Writing Automation With the Joysticks

Punching automation writing in or out works the same with the joysticks as with other controls, with three additional features.

To punch automation without touching the joystick:

1. Press the **In** button next to the joystick.
   At the button press, the joystick behaves the same as if it were in Latch. It will continue writing its position until punched out.
- In this mode, to punch automation out do one of these:
   o Touch the joystick.
   o Press the **In** button again.

To punch automation out while in Touch or Touch/Latch without letting go of the joystick:

- Press the **In** button next to the joystick.

Using Pickup Mode

Unlike most other surface controls, the joysticks report their actual physical position. Because they are not motorized, that position may not match the underlying automation. When a joystick is touched, automation data will instantaneously jump to its physical position. This can cause some undesirable jumps or hiccups. This may be mitigated by using Pickup Mode. In this mode, automation writing will not begin until the current joystick position matches the underlying automation position.

To punch joystick automation in using Pickup Mode:

1. Activate the **Pickup Mode** button on the MJM.
2. While playing, the current joystick position is displayed as a white outlined circle. The underlying automation position is displayed as a red dot.
3. Touching the joystick, move the white circle (or wait with it in position) until the red and white circles coincide.
4. The automation indicators will flash red and the joystick's moves will continue to be written.

To punch automation out while in Write, Latch, or Pickup Mode, do one of these:

- Press the **F** button on the MJM Track Controls.
- Press the **F** button on the fader section.

Other MJM Controls
Controlling Other Panning Parameters

While the joysticks give the mixer great control of the panning position, they do not easily allow control of Divergence, Center Percentage, or LFE levels. These parameters can be controlled via the MJM's Knob Cluster. When the panning function is selected, the parameters of the last-attentioned track are also available on the Attention Track knobs.

To assign a pan parameter to the Pan Knob Cluster:

- Use the nudge buttons (◀ or ▶) at the bottom of the Knob Cluster to navigate to the desired panning parameter.

The parameter name and setting will display in the Knob Cluster's OLED.

The last-selected parameter for a track can be recalled to the Pan Knob Cluster when the track is attentioned to a joystick. Check **Settings > User > Knobs/Remember Joystick Knobs by Track**.

Constraining Joysticks to Horizontal or Vertical

By default, each joystick controls both the horizontal (X) or vertical (Y) axes, but either axis may be disabled, constraining control to only one. Disabling both X and Y axes will disable the joystick's movement, though its static position may be written when automation is punched for that joystick.

Joystick controls

To activate or deactivate the X or Y axis of a joystick:

• Press **Mode/X** or **Alt1/Y** buttons on the MJM.

Linking Stereo Pairs

When a stereo track is assigned to the two sections of the MJM, they may be unlinked to allow independent pan adjustments to be made to each. The **Link** and **Invert** buttons are outlined in gray to indicate that they only operate on stereo tracks.

To unlink or re-link a stereo pair:

• Toggle the **Link** (⊂⊃) button.

When a stereo track is linked in the two joysticks, it can be set to Invert, which causes the two panners to work in mirror image to one-another.

To invert or un-invert a stereo pair:

• Toggle the Invert (↔) button.

For more advanced features of this module, check Avid's S6 Guide.

Chapter 17
Snapshots

One of the most mysterious of features in Pro Tools and in the Avid S6 is Snapshots. They allow users to capture and save some or all mix settings at a timeline location and apply (punch) them at any location in your mix. Capture and punching work much like Automation Preview of Pro Tools, except that 48 captured previews (Snapshots) can be retained.

How Snapshots Work
- A group of settings are captured into the Capture Buffer – either All settings, or selected settings. When *selected* settings are to be captured, only settings that are writing automation, primed for writing automation or which are in the Preview buffer will be captured. When *all* settings are to be captured, their write-state is unimportant: if they are enabled they will be captured; all automation in all tracks.
- Once captured, settings are saved to one of six Snap# slots on one of the eight Soft Key Snapshots pages.
- To recall a Snapshot, a Snap# is selected and Punch Capture on a Soft Key page is pressed. If all settings were captured, they will all be applied with Punch Capture.
- Parameters may be excluded from the capture or the punch process by disabling them in the Automation window (**Shift+1**)

Navigating to Snapshot Soft Key Pages
There are multiple paths to the Snapshots Soft Key controls. Here are three.

DOI: 10.4324/9781003111801–21

Table 17.1 Soft Key pages and how to get to them

Command	Page	Path to Soft Key Page
Enable automation types	Automation 3	**Shift + 1**
Preview, Punch Preview, Capture, Snapshots	Automation 2	**Shift + 1** to reveal **Snapshot** navigation button
Capture, Capture All, Save Snapshot, Rename Snapshot, Snap#	Snapshots 1–8	**Shift + 0 / Extras/Snapshots**

Capturing and Saving Snapshots

To capture a Snapshot of selected automation:

1. Turn on **Allow Latch Prime in Stop** using **Pro Tools > Setup > Preferences... > Mixing/Automation**.
2. On Soft Key page **Automation 3** select all automation types that you wish to capture.
3. Set all tracks that you want included in the Snapshot to **Latch** automation mode.
4. Adjust controls and touch any already-adjusted controls. This primes their values for writing.
5. On a **Snapshots** Soft Key page press **Capture.** All primed controls will be copied to the Capture Buffer.

> This whole procedure feels odd to me because it requires you to make settings without auditioning their effect. Let's put this into a more likely workflow. Suppose you are adjusting several automation parameters in several tracks, and you know you will want to apply the same settings elsewhere as well.
>
> Use Preview mode as usual. Audition and adjust until you achieve the desired results. Punch and apply the preview settings, then copy those settings into the Capture Buffer and save it to one of the Snapshot slots.

To capture a Snapshot of Previewed automation:

1. On **Automation 3** select all automation types that you wish to capture.
2. Set any tracks which you want to capture into an automation writing mode; **Touch, Touch/Latch** or **Latch**.[1]

---

1. Write mode will serve to capture automation settings, but it will also write while auditioning, which is rarely desirable.

3. On **Automation 2** Soft Key page press **Preview** to activate Preview Mode.
4. Audition and adjust parameter settings on the desired tracks. Touch any already-adjusted controls to include them in the preview.
5. When settings are optimal, on **Automation 2** or a **Snapshots** page or in the Pro Tools Automation window, press **Capture**.

Other Options

Another possible scenario is that you will capture a Snapshot of *all* enabled automation settings in the session at the current location – to be applied later. This is simpler because it does not involve creating the settings to be captured. It is dangerous because it captures *all* enabled automation of all active tracks.

To capture a snapshot of all enabled automation:

1. On Soft Key page Automation 3 select all automation types that you wish to capture.
2. Go to a location where you want all automation captured.
3. On a Snapshots Soft Key page do one of these:
   • Press **Capture All** on Soft Key page Snapshots 1.
   • Press **Opt/Win** (modifier key) + Capture on Soft Key page Automation 2.
   • Press **Option + Capture** in the Pro Tools Automation Window.

Storing Captured Snapshots

Soft Key pages Snapshots 1–8 contain 48 Snapshot slots. Occupied slots are gray. If you navigate past page 8, you cannot navigate directly back to it. That is annoying. You have the option to name saved Snapshots, but that name does not appear anywhere that I can see. That is weird.

Saving a Snapshot to an occupied Snapshot slot will overwrite it with no warning dialog. That could be aggravating.

To save captured Snapshots:

1. On a **Snapshots** Soft Key page press **Save Snapshot** then select the desired **Snap#**. The slot changes to gray.
2. For the fun of it, press **Rename Snapshot** then **Snap#**. Type in a name using the workstation keyboard.

Recalling Snapshots

Recalling and Applying Snapshots

Recalling a Snapshot puts it into the Capture Buffer, where it may be applied in the same way the Preview buffer is applied.

To recall a Snapshot:

1. Navigate to the desired Soft Key **Snapshots** page.
2. Be sure that all automation which you want to receive Snapshots is enabled.
3. Press the **Snap#** that you want to apply. It will flash.

The Capture Buffer will be loaded with the Snapshot. It may be applied in any of the ways the Preview would be applied, using Punch Capture in the place of Punch Preview.

Chapter 18

Expand Faders

The S6 is a very expanding mix surface.

We explored Strip Expand Knobs, which allow users to spill parameters of functions from one track into the 32 knob clusters of the Knob Module(s).

We visited VCA Expand Knobs, which allow users to spill VCA GMs from a VCA Master into the 32 knob clusters of the Knob Module.

We looked at Attention Expand Knobs, which allow users to spill function parameters into the Attention Track knobs.

And we tried out VCA Attention Expand Knobs, which allow VCA Masters to be spilled into the Attention Track knobs.

Now it is time to see what Expand Faders are all about.

This expand feature was saved for last because – well – most of us can mix well without it. Expand Faders are not useless, but they can further confuse the learning process. Now that you know how those other expand features work, this new one will be a quick one to understand and master.

Using Expand Faders

Expand Fader mode allows you map specific parameters of a plug-in (or other functions) onto up to two banks of the eight faders of the fader section of the chassis section.

DOI: 10.4324/9781003111801–22

The mapping can be saved (in User Preferences) and automatically invoked when a function is expanded to the Knob Module.

Any plug-in can be mapped to faders, but you should ask yourself if it really helps you to have some of the settings of a reverb or a ring modulator spilled onto two banks of eight faders. Expand Faders will work best with slider-oriented plug-ins, such as Waves WNS, SA-2 or FabFilter Pro-MB. When applied to the right function, this is an excellent feature.

McDSP® SA-2 with expanded faders applied

To use Expand Faders, you must first create an Expand Fader map for each function you want to expand. It will work for all instances of that function.

To create an Expand Fader map:

1. Select the desired function on the Process section.
2. Hold the Attention (△) button on the desired track, and press **Exp** button in the Process section of that track.
   The **Exp** button will flash blue; the **Clear** button will light red; the currently selected function will populate the Knob Module, and the faders should drop to ∞.
   If any parameters have been previously mapped, they will appear on the faders.
3. Touch a parameter in the Knob Module that you want to map to a fader. That knob will flash.
4. Touch the fader onto which you want to map that parameter. The fader will populate with that parameter, and the knob will stop flashing.
5. To clear a fader assignment, tap any unlit knob of the Knob Module, then touch the fader you want to clear.
6. To clear all current mapping, press the **Clear** button on the strip.
7. To change a parameter mapping, repeat steps 3 and 4.
8. Continue mapping any additional parameters; first touch the knob, then touch the fader.
9. To create a second page of Expanded Faders for this function, press the lit **User 2** button in the Modifier keys. A second page of faders will appear. Return to Page 1 with **User 1** button.
10. When mapping is complete, press **Exp** button again and the mapping is stored.

To recall an Expand Fader map, do one of these:

- To automatically recall Expanded Faders whenever a mapped function is expanded:
  a. Set **User Settings > Surface > Strips > Auto Expand Functions/Faders** to **On**.
  b. Press **Exp**.
- To use Expanded Fader on demand:
  a. Set **User Settings > Surface > Strips > Auto Expand Functions/Faders** to **off.**
  b. Press and hold **Exp** button for about 2 seconds and the faders will expand.

If no Expanded Fader mapping is saved for the current plug-in, the **Exp** button on the LED turns blue.

When Expand Faders are active, the fader section of that track is hijacked. You cannot use the volume fader, nor the **Solo**, **Mute**, automation (**F**) or Trim (**M**) buttons.

- One strategy is to always set these controls before entering Expand Mode.
- Another strategy is to attention the track so that those buttons are available on the Attention Track fader section.
- The attentioning must be evoked before entering Expand Fader mode.

With **System Settings > General > Preferences/Expand Faders** checked **On**, the Expand Fader maps will be saved with the session (as well as with Title files).

The mapping will be saved in whichever way you are saving User Preferences (*see "User Preferences" on page 32*).

Chapter 19

Making Selections in the Pro Tools Timeline

What are Selections?

If you have been working with Pro Tools for more than a few minutes you have made Selections. When mixing on the S6, controlling the location and duration of the Selection allows you to set areas for loop-auditioning or for the application of **write to selected...** when utilizing Preview and Punch Preview features of Pro Tools.

Managing the Selection is commonly done using Mouse and Keyboard on the Pro Tools screen, but the S6 has some very slick methods to easily create or alter the Selection. Nonetheless, if you are quick and familiar with Pro Tools, you will probably be more comfortable making selections with a mouse on the Pro Tools screen.

A Selection occurs in Pro Tools when an area of the timeline is highlighted. The **Start** and **End** will have different values, and the **Length** will have a value greater than 0.

A Selection in Pro Tools

When creating and using Selections, it is best to turn off **Insertion Follows Playback** in the Pro Tools section, either in the **Options** menu, or by de-selecting it in the edit window header. Otherwise, the Selection is lost at the end of any play cycle.

Insertion follows Playback

The crankiest issue when trying to use Selections on the S6 is that there is no indication on the surface of *where* the current Selection is in the Pro Tools session. You must view it in the Pro Tools window.

DOI: 10.4324/9781003111801-23

All the following methods will change the location of the Selection in Pro Tools but will not move clips or automation.

In and Out vs. Start and End?

In reference to Selections, the S6 uses the terms "In" and "Out" where Pro Tools uses "Start" and "End." The Start of a Selection is called the In point. The end of a Selection is the Out point.

How to Clear a Selection:

- Press the ↓ key, just above the numeric keypad. The Selection will clear, leaving the insertion point at the playhead.
- If pressed while playing, the insertion point will be left at the point in the timeline where the key was pressed.

Creating Selections with Mark In and Mark Out

Combined with the Jog Wheel, the two **Mark** buttons in the Locate Buttons section of the Automation Module help you set the start and end points of the Selection. The behavior of this method is not intuitive, but once you get used to it, is very quick to use.

Mark In allows you to change the start (In) point of the Selection.

Locates buttons – Mark In and Out

Press **Mark In** and turn the Jog Wheel left. The In point of the Selection is drawn left from the insertion point.

With insertion at the Out point press **Mark In**

Turn the Jog Wheel left to extend the **In** point left

Press **Mark In** again to exit the Selection process.

Mark Out allows you to change the end (Out) point of the Selection.

Press **Mark Out** and turn the Jog Wheel right. The Selection is drawn right from the insertion point.

With the insertion at the In point press **Mark Out**	Turn the Jog Wheel right to extend the **Out** point right

Press **Mark Out** again to exit the Selection process.

To create a Selection when the insertion point is at the desired In point:

1. Press **Mark Out**. Its LED will light.
2. Turn the Jog Wheel right until you reach the desired Out point.
3. Press **Mark Out** again to exit Selection process.

To create a Selection when the insertion point is at the desired Out point.

1. Press **Mark In**. Its LED will light.
2. Turn the Jog Wheel left until you reach the desired In point.
3. Press **Mark In** again to exit Selection process.

These two methods work great when the insertion point is sitting right where you want either the start or end to be. But if they are *close* to the desired start or end point, there is a clever and quick alternative.

To create a Selection when the insertion point is near the desired In point:

1. Press **Mark In**. Its LED will light.
2. Turn the Jog Wheel right until the insertion point reaches the desired end point of the Selection.

3. The insertion point will slide to the right, but a Selection will not be made.
4. Turn the Jog Wheel to the left, and a Selection will be made starting from the right-most position, extending back as the insertion point moves left.
5. Press **Mark In** again to exit Selection process.

| With the insertion point near the In point press **Mark In** | Turn the Jog Wheel right until the Out point is reached. No Selection is made. | Turn the Jog Wheel left until the In point is reached and a Selection is made |

To create a Selection when the insertion point is near the desired Out point:

1. Press **Mark Out**. Its LED will light.
2. Turn the Jog Wheel to the left until the insertion point reaches the In point of your desired Selection.
3. The insertion will slide to the left, but a Selection will not be made. If the insertion point was already at the left-most point of your desired Selection, DO NOTHING.
4. Turn the Jog Wheel to the right, and a Selection will be made starting from the left-most position, extending as the insertion point moves right.

| With the insertion point near the Out point press **Mark Out** | Turn the Jog Wheel left until the In point is reached. No Selection is made. | Turn the Jog Wheel right until the In point is reached and a Selection is made. |

When a Selection already exists, the In- or Out-points can be adjusted.

Changing a Selection

To adjust the start or end of a Selection with Mark In or Mark Out and the Jog Wheel:

1. Press **Mark In** to adjust the start of a Selection, or **Mark Out** to adjust the end of a Selection.
2. Turn the Jog Wheel to adjust the start or end of a Selection.
3. Press **Mark In** or **Mark Out** again to exit Selection Adjustment Mode.

To move an entire Selection left or right with the Jog Wheel do one of these:

- Press **Trim**. The button's LED will light.
- Press **amShift** + **Move Selection**.

The Jog Wheel buttons

Turning the Jog Wheel left or right will move the Selection.

Press **Trim** or **amShift** + **Move Selection** to deactivate this mode.

To restore the last (lost) Selection:

- Press **Shift** (Modifier key) + ↓.

To move the Selection into the track above or below:

- To move the Selection upwards, press ⌘ + |◄ on the Transport keys.
- To move the Selection downwards, press ⌘ + ►| on the Transport keys.

To extend the Selection into the track above or below:

- To extend the Selection upward press Option + ►| on the Transport keys.
- To extend the Selection downward press Option + |◄ on the Transport keys.

You may notice that these two command groups behave differently from one-another. I would expect that using the ◄ button would move or extend upwards, and that the ► button would move or extend downwards, but it is not consistent. Do not be surprised when you try it.

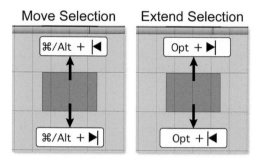

Move or extend Selections to adjacent tracks.

Chapter 20

Colors and Lights

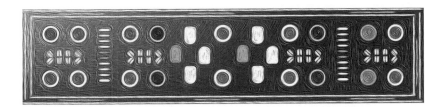

Signals

The S6 uses color in many places to inform the mixer of the assignments of various controls. Mixers who remember the meaning of these colors can seem to hold a more magical grasp of the S6, so let's just keep this between you and me. Recognizing that a control is assigned to EQ rather than Dynamics without having to read the little words on the surface may liberate you in an indescribable way. Or not.

Channel Strips

If a color has been assigned to a track in the Pro Tools session, that color will be displayed on the modifier key at the bottom of the channel. The color does not respond to any function of the modifier key; the color is simply informative.

Function Colors

A control which is assigned a function will light with a standard color. For example, if EQ is spilled to the knob section, those knobs will light magenta.

Table 20.1 Function Colors

Color	Function	Function	Color
Blue	Pan	Bus Outputs	Gold
Gold	Bus Outputs	Green	Dynamics
Green	Dynamics	EQ	Magenta
Light Yellow	Sends	Groups	Orange
Magenta	EQ	Red	Input
Orange	Groups	Input	Red
Red	Input	Inserts	Turquoise
Turquoise	Inserts	Sends	Light Yellow
Sorted by Color		Sorted by Function	

DOI: 10.4324/9781003111801-24

In cases where there may be more than one function of the same type inserted on a track, the Master Module knobs will light in a slight variation of the standard color to differentiate one function from the other. For example, if a 7-Band EQ3 and a NF575 are inserted in the same track, the Master Module knobs will show slightly different variations of magenta depending on which of those two functions is assigned to the knobs.

Note that both Pan and User (Instrument Plug-Ins) are blue. For most movie mixing situations these two types will not be used simultaneously, but keep in mind that they *could* show up at the same time.

Bank and Nudge Switch Element Colors

When Spill Zones are being used, the color of the Bank and Nudge button LEDs on the Master Module will indicate what type of element is spilled into them. The color of the Menu buttons of the tracks occupying the spill will show the same color.

Table 20.2 Bank/Nudge Colors

Element Type	L Spill/R Spill LED	Channel Strip Menu LED
VCA Master	Dark Green	Dark Green
VCA GM	Dark Green	Light Green
Layouts	Dark Blue	Dark Blue
Track Type	Pink	Pink
Workstation	Light Blue	Light Blue

Soft Key Page Headers

The headers of Soft Key Pages are color coded by their type or function. These colors are not necessarily consistent with LED and control colors, Avid does not have a hard reference for these colors, and if a user creates their own Soft Key Pages, the colors may be chosen without regard to a standard. But for what it is worth, here are some common page colors. There may be many more yet, but they haven't been discovered.

Table 20.3 Some Soft Key header colors

Type	Color	Type	Color
Automation	Red	Clip Fx	Green
Home Screen Prefs	Dark Red	Playlist Commands	Green
Session Management	Blue	Edit Commands	Green

Type	Color	Type	Color
Groups, Extras	Purple	Memory Locations	Acid Green
Pro Tools Commands	Purple	Banking	Aqua
Midi	Purple	Machine Control	Gray
Track Preferences	Violet	Console Settings	Gray
Workstation Settings	Orange	Surface Controls	Teal

Flashing Lights

The Automation Mode (**F**) button lights red when automation is armed, such as with Latch Prime, and it flashes when automation is being written on this track.

The LEDs next to the Automation Mode (F) button indicate its automation mode status:

- No Light = Off   Green=Read   Red = Any write mode.
- Flashing red when stopped means Latch Prime is activated and primed.
- Flashing red when rolling forward means automation is being written.

Module Status on Startup

> The likelihood of you ever needing to use this is low, but you will impress everyone when you wave this little tip around in the engineer's lunchroom.

An obscure feature using color and lights tells users the status of modules as the console starts up. On each module, a specified LED will light if the module has power. Its color will indicate whether that module is claimed in the current Surface Configuration.

- Unlit = Module is not powered.
- Purple = Module is ready to use.
- Yellow/Orange = Module is powered, but not assigned to the current Surface Configuration.

At the completion of Start-up, this light will clear on all claimed modules After Start-up, the orange-yellow LED will remain lit on modules that are not assigned. If the entire module is dark, probably no power.

Table 20.4 Module Start-up status indicators

Module	Location	Button LED
Automation Module	Attention Fader	Track Color (Modifier Key)
Fader Module	Strip 1	Track Color (Modifier Key)
Knob Module	Strip 1	Back button
Process Module	Strip 1	Back button
Master Module	Lower Left	Back button
Master Joystick Module	Lower Left	Back button
Master Post Module	Strip 1	Track Color (Modifier Key)

Chapter 21
What is Next?

We have explored all the basic and intermediate mixing tools of the Avid S6 console. There is little that you cannot do using these tools in any format from monaural thru 7.1 surround.

There are, of course, more features to extend the capabilities into Atmos and other formats. There are also more features of the S6 which have not been covered. With the fundamentals under your control, you can explore them on your own.

Here are some of the more interesting tools you may need (or want) to experience.

Editing on the Surface
Most of us who work in this environment do our editing on the workstation and our mixing on the S6 surface. Avid has provided some interesting and mostly basic tools for editing from the console, so why not check them out. They may come in handy.

Using Attention Expand Zones
Additional Track Modules and Knob Modules can be installed into the S6 frame and used as targets for spilling of parameters for custom purposes. If your system has any of these, check out what you can do with them.

Using Multiple Workstations
The S6 can function as an elaborate switch, swapping control from one source workstation or application to another. Its true power lies in the ability to build track layouts which are sourced from those multiple workstations or applications. Without switching, a mixer can build a mixing desk that accesses all the tracks of all available connected sources. Using VCA Masters and GMs and Track Layouts, organization of tracks can be vastly simplified, giving the mixer tremendous power over a complex mix.

DOI: 10.4324/9781003111801-25

Using Multiple Post Modules

When two or more mixers are contributing to a complex mix at the same time, using multiple Post Modules can allow seamless workflows.

Customize Soft Key Pages

The S6 allows the creation of shortcut keys to do nearly anything, so creating custom Soft Key pages gives a mixer quick access to complicated S6 commands.

Customize Post Module Buttons

Some of the buttons on the Post Module are customizable. Creating shortcut keys and assigning them to the Post Module can optimize the mixer's workflow.

Customizing Jog Wheel Buttons

This, too, is possible if you can find the instructions for it.

ATMOS Panning with the Joystick Module and the Touchscreen Function Editor

There is a lot to learn here, but beyond the scope of this book.

Assigning Unconventional Parameters to the Joysticks.

All the demos show this feature which allows you to assign any parameter to the X and Y of the joysticks. Try it out and see if you can find anything truly useful or creative.

Appendix I

A Collection of Disconnected Facts and Features

Lorem ipsum dolor sit amet, consectetuer adipiscing elit, sed diam nonummy nibh euismod tincidunt ut laoreet dolore magna aliquam erat volutpat. Ut wisi enim ad minim veniam, quis nostrud exerci tation ullamcorper suscipit lobortis nisl ut aliquip ex ea commodo consequat. Duis autem vel eum iriure dolor in hendrerit in vulputate velit esse molestie consequat, vel illum dolore eu feugiat nulla facilisis at vero eros et accumsan et iusto odio dignissim qui blandit praesent luptatum zzril delenit augue duis dolore te feugait nulla facilisi. Lorem ipsum dolor sit amet, consectetuer adipiscing elit, sed diam nummy nibh euismod tincidunt ut laoreet dolore magna aliquam erat volutpat. Ut wisi enim ad minim veniam, quis nostrud exerci tation ullamcorper suscipit lobortis nisl ut aliquip ex ea commodo consequat. Lorem ipsum dolor sit amet, consectetuer adipiscing elit, sed diam nonummy nibh euismod tincidunt ut laoreet dolore magna aliquam erat volutpat. Ut wisi enim ad minim veniam, quis nostrud exerci tation

A Bit More on the Monitoring Screen and XMon

The XMon unit may control analog monitoring paths from the S6 to your studio. It is controlled via the XMon software by settings made on the S6 surface and /or the Monitoring Screen.

The S6 plays well using XMON, AX32, or MTRX (using DADman application) and possibly other monitoring hardware, so check with your studio engineers to determine which system is being used. Whichever it is, the controlling software must be configured properly and focused to the S6. For this section, "XMON" will refer to any of the monitor hardware.

The Monitoring screen

Speaker Output Selection

The XMon unit has four 25-pin connectors. Three are outputs and one is input/output. They *should* be connected as follows:

Main Speakers:	Up to 7.1 "Mix" output channels
Alt Speakers:	Up to 7.1 "Alt Speaker" output channels
Cue Outputs:	Up to four stereo "Cue" output channels
TB/LB/Util:	Talkback, Listenback, AFL inputs, and Mini Speakers

To select output speaker sets on the Master Module surface:

- Press **Main Spkrs**, **Alt 1 Spkrs**, or **Alt 2 Spkrs** (mini speakers) on the S6 surface Studio/Talk controls area, on the lower right of the Master Module.

Each of these speaker selections has a separate level setting, displayed on the OLED when they are active.

Not all systems will have Alt speakers or Mini speakers installed. Some speaker selections may not be wired to their full capacity (7.1 or Stereo). Check with your engineer regarding your installation.

To turn individual speakers on or off:

- Select or de-select speakers in the speaker section at the bottom of the Monitoring Screen.

From the Monitoring Screen, you may make some important selections and adjustments to what is being heard.

Audio Sources

Across the top 1/3 is the Source Scroller. While up to 16 different source devices can feed into the monitors, usually no more than eight are visible. The source devices are wired into the system, and labels may describe what they are, or may not… Check with your engineer to learn which buttons in the Source Scroller represent which devices.

Cue Paths (Monitor A, B, C, D)

The left Attention Track knobs control dedicated stereo cue output paths. These cue paths are typically used for creating monitor mixes, cueing mixes for ADR or foley artists, or other custom monitor mixes. The destination of these paths is dependent on your studio's installation, so check with the engineer to learn where each cue path leads.

The level of the first two cue paths can be adjusted from the Studio/Talk area of the Lower Master Module (MonA and MonB). All four cue path levels can be adjusted or muted from the Monitor A–Monitor D knobs of the Monitoring Screen.

Each cue path can be assigned one or more sources from the Source Select area of the Monitor Screen.

To assign source audio to a cue path:

1. Touch the Name Box next to the encoder display on a cue path.
   The Source Select area will highlight any sources that are already assigned to the cue path.

2. Touch any available source within to the Source Select area to toggle its assignment to that cue path.

Local settings can change the selection behavior between Sum and Intercancel.

Talkback and Listenback
(Talk and Coms buttons)

Up to two microphones may be installed to allow the mixer to communicate with people in a different room.

A Talkback microphone may be installed on the console, its output sent to a headphone feed or recording-room speaker (or anywhere). The destination is dependent on your installation.

A Listenback microphone may be installed anywhere in your studio spaces. It feeds into the control room monitor when active. The source is dependent on your installation.

Volume controls for Talkback and Listenback are in the Control Room section of the Lower Master Module as well as on the right-side Attention Track knobs when the Monitoring Screen is displaying.

Talkback and Listenback have three modes: Normal (momentary), Latch, and Auto. The mode is selected in **Monitoring Screen > Local Options (✿)**.

When Talkback or Listenback is active, the Studio/Talk output is dimmed by the dim amount setting. *If monitor levels have suddenly dropped, check the* Talk *and* Coms *buttons – maybe they are latched on.*

Talkback and Listenback are activated using the Talk and (of course) Coms buttons in the Studio/Talk section of the Lower Master Module.

Using Talkback Modes
To talk momentarily:
• Press and hold the Talk button.

The mic operates while you hold the Talkback button.

To Latch the Talk Button
• Press the Talk button for less than ½ second.

The mic toggles between latched off and latched on.

To Talk using Auto Talkback:

- When enabled in local settings (*see above*) the Talkback remains on except during record or playback of the DAW.

> *The Talk button LED indicates that the console microphone is active, so be careful what you say when that LED is lit.*

Using Listenback Modes
To listen momentarily:

- Press and hold the **Coms** button.

To latch the Listenback mode:

- Press the **Coms** button for less than a half second: the mic toggles between latched off and latched on.

To listen using Auto Listenback:

- When enabled in local settings (*see above*) Listenback remains on except during record or playback.

To use Listenback (Normal or Latch enabled):

When active, Listenback mode dims the Studio/Talk output by the dim amount and activates the Listenback mic.

The **Coms** button activates Listenback mode. Its LED lights when active.

Talk and Listenback Levels
Level controls for Talk and Listenback may be accessed in two places:

- When the Monitoring Screen is active, the top two Attention Track knobs on the right side of the touchscreen control their volume.
- In the Control Room section of the Lower Master Module, the knobs next to **Coms** button and **Talk** buttons adjust Listenback and Talkback levels respectively.

Useful Soft Key Pages

Preferences   Shift + Star (★)

- Preference settings for S6 and Pro Tools.

Automation 1   Shift + 0,1, 2, 3, 5

- Automation modes **write**, **Touch**, **Latch**, etc.
- **Do to All** and **Do to Selected**.
- **Automation Suspend** and **Automation Off**.
- Page Menu – menu of some other pages available. Press to open that page.

Page Menu   Reached from Automation 1

- Meters – change meter types; gain reduction display functions; enable mini-meter display of sends in Pro Tools.

Automation 2   Shift + 0,1,2,3

- Preview, Punch Preview, and Write Automation commands. Access to Snapshot pages if you press Control modifier key.

Automation 3   Shift + 1

- **Automation Enable commands** – found on the Pro Tools Automation window but arranged differently from the familiar layout of the window.

Automation 4   Shift + 1 or bank from Automation 1,2,3

- **Automation Prime in Stop**, Automation Edit commands **write to Current**, **Glide to Current**, etc.

Session Management 1   Shift + 0,1, 4, 6, 9

- **Snapshots** – Capture or recall up to 48 snapshots. Use the Right and Left navigation buttons to move to different layers of this page.

Extras 1   Shift + 0

- **Mem Locators Page** – Access up to 100 locators.

Banking (Officially "Spill Zones")   **Shift + Enter**

- Three sets of buttons control banking for Banking Mode, L Spill, and R Spill zones – all on two pages.

Memory Locations   **Mem Loc or Shift + 0**

- Access up to 100 locators.

Showing Hidden Tracks Without Un-Hiding Them

Even though some tracks may have been hidden for a good reason, you may have a good reason to ignore their hidden status and display them anyway – without changing their status. Go to **Settings > User > Surface > Strips / Show Hidden Tracks**. This state can be enabled or disabled for Banking Mode, Layout Mode or VCA Spill mode, independent of one another. Tracks will have these attributes:

Track Indicators	Track Status
Fully lit.	Active, shown and unmuted.
Track name is dimmed, no track number shown.	Active, hidden, unmuted.
Entire strip is dimmed, no track number shown.	Active, hidden, muted.
Entire strip dimmed, track name dimmed slightly, track number shown.	Muted.
"@" appears before its group or I/O assignments.	Track is inactive.

> Except for the "@" and "Fully Lit" indicators the visual distinction between the others is so obscure as to be nearly useless. The rule is, if a track on the display module is darker than others, it is possibly not playing, unless it is only hidden.

Copying All Automation from One Track to Another

Copying an audio clip from one track to another will copy all its automation along with the clip, but sometimes we need to copy only the automation without changing the audio.

Unfortunately, the S6 does not offer this option directly, but it can be done in the Pro Tools window or with clever manipulation of the Selection controls and Pro Tools keyboard. I recommend that you just use the Pro Tools keyboard.

To copy and paste all automation of a track using the Pro Tools Edit window:

1. In the Automation Window (**window > Automation or +4**) assure that all parameter types that you want to copy are selected.
2. Set at least one of the source tracks to display any automation lane, such as volume (**control + option + minus** (-) on Pro Tools keyboard).
3. Select the area in the track(s) and timeline that you want to copy.
   - Automation of more than one track may be copied at one time. Multiple tracks need not be contiguous.
   - If there is no Selection, the automation copy command will not work.
4. Type **control + command + c** on the Pro Tools keyboard.
5. Select the point in the destination track(s) where you want to paste all automation.
   - If you copied automation from more than one track, select the same number of tracks. Selecting fewer tracks will paste to fewer tracks. Selecting more tracks will not paste beyond the number of copied tracks.
   - Multiple tracks need not be contiguous. Automation will paste into multiple tracks in the order they were copied.
6. Type **control + command + v** on the Pro Tools keyboard.
7. Regardless of the length of the paste selection, only the entire length of the copied automation will be pasted to the selected track(s).

Changing OLED Display Options

Go to **Settings > User > Surface > Strips** to change options for the Fader Section OLEDs.
- **Show Track Number**
- **Show Workstation Number**
- **Show Timed Fader Values and**
- **Fader Value Timeout**

Alternatively, these settings can be changed on the Soft Key pads. Press **Shift** (modifier key) **+ Star** (*). Press **Shift + 0** to return Soft Key pads to their default state.

Assigning an Assignable Knob

Yes, there is a way to assign those assignable knobs.

To assign a parameter to an assignable knob:

1. Hold the **Back** (◢▬◣) button on the desired track and press **any** of the Function Select buttons of the Process Section.
2. Use the ◄ or ► buttons on either side of the **Back** button to select the plug-in.

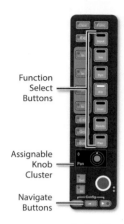

Function
Select
Buttons

Assignable
Knob
Cluster

Navigate
Buttons

Assignable
Knob Cluster

3. Use the ◀ or ▶ buttons to nudge each parameter of the selected function to the knob.
4. The **Back** button will navigate up one level.
5. OLED above the knob will display the function parameter that is currently being controlled by the knob, as well as its current value (*see "Knob Cluster Behavior" on page 47 for more details*).

Use the **All** button on the Master Module to assign the same parameter to all assignable knobs. Tracks which do not contain the same insert will not be assigned.

Focusing an Application or Workstation

This book does not delve too deeply into the use of multiple applications or workstations, but it is possible that intermediate users will encounter this feature. More detailed information is available in the S6 Guide. Search "To open the workstations page."

To focus a workstation or application using Soft Key pads:

1. On the Master Module, press **WS**.
   - Connected and available workstations and applications will be displayed on a Soft Key pad.
2. Press the button next to the desired workstation or application.

Press **Close** on the Soft Key pad to release the Soft Key page to other uses.

To focus a workstation or application when attentioned:

1. Navigate the Touchscreen to **Settings > User > Surface > Attention**
2. Check "**Focus Workstation of Most Recently Attentioned Track**."

Locking Transport Controls to an Application or Workstation

When using multiple workstations or applications, the Transport Controls can be locked to one of them to give consistent control.

To Lock Transport Controls to an Application/Workstation:

1. Focus the desired application/workstation.
2. Press the Setup button on the Automation Module, to the right of the Transport Controls. Its LED will light.

Jog Wheel LEDs

Although the jog wheel is surrounded by LEDs, they do not light.

Momentary Group Suspend

To change any control which is currently a member of a non-VCA group without changing other group members:

1. Hold **Ctrl** modifier key.
2. Adjust the desired control or controls.

All controls return to group control behavior when **Ctrl** is released.

VCA Masters vs Aux Tracks vs Grouped Tracks

Do not confuse VCA groups with other grouped tracks or with the use of Aux tracks.

VCA Masters operate only the volume of their member tracks. They act the same as your finger on the member track faders. They can raise faders to their topmost level only (+12 dB). Individual faders in a VCA group can be adjusted independently of other GMs.

Grouped tracks can link a spectrum of controls of all grouped tracks, which can include inserts, sends, bypass, solo, mute and more (set in the Pro Tools Modify Groups window). Adjusting any linked control of one grouped track can change that control of all grouped tracks.

Aux tracks act as audio accumulators: the audio paths of all tracks that are assigned to an Aux track merge together. Any processing within an Aux track is applied to all audio which is passing through it. Using the Aux track fader, the level of audio passing through an Aux track can be raised 12 dB above the incoming level.

What's So Bad About Auto Insert?

Auto Insert is a Pro Tools feature which automatically instantiates an EQ or Dyn plug-in into a track if it does not already have one. Auto Insert is triggered by pressing Dyn or EQ in the Process section of a channel strip.

The non-creative aspects of mixing are best served by organization and consistency. Most polished mixers will pre-instantiate, enable automation for and anchor the automation of plug-ins, sends, returns, and other processes. During the mixing, if they need to instantiate additional tools they will do so deliberately and carefully to avoid surprises which might sabotage their mix.

Having the system adding processes into mix channels is the opposite of deliberate and careful management of the mixing resources, so should be avoided.

Console Keystroke Oddities

Interesting? Dangerous? Silly? You decide.

- Each fader section and the upper Master Module has a Swap button. These buttons have contextually varying uses, but they never Swap anything.
- In the Location section of the Automation Module, below the Location display.
  - ○ **mmShift + Save** will execute **Save As…** on the workstation session.
  - ○ ↓ is the equilavent of the down-arrow key on the DAW Keyboard. It will place the insertion at the current playhead position and clear any current selection.
  - ○ ↓ **+ Shift** (modifier key) will restore the last (lost) selection.
- When there is a selection in Pro Tools:
  - ○ **Consol Clip** will consolidate a selection, the same as pressing **Shift + option + 3** on Pro Tools keyboard.
  - ○ **Trim Clip** will truncate any clips within the selection, the same as pressing ⌘ **+ T** on Pro Tools keyboard.
- Pressing either of the lower two **Setup** buttons on Monitor control area of the Lower Master Module will cause the Monitoring page to appear on the Touchscreen.
- **WARNING:** The upper-most **Setup** button on the Control Room area of the Lower Master Module locks or unlocks the monitor application (XMon or DADman) from the S6. On startup, the S6 locks to the first monitor application that it sees. Unlocking it allows you to select a different monitor application or workstation.
- **mmShift + 3** begins recording on all record-armed tracks.
- **mmShift + ◀ Mixer** toggles the mix window of workstation screen.
  mmShift + ▶ Close closes the front-most window of the workstation screen.

Automation Mode Status LEDs

Any automation-enabled control on the surface which has an LED will show its automation status via its color and behavior. This results in a lot of lit or blinking LEDs.

- **Red LED on-**   The control is set to an automation-writing mode (Touch, Latch, Touch/Latch, or Write).
- **Red LED off-**   The control set to a non-writing automation mode, or if the green LED is flashing, the control is in a Preview state.
- **Red LED flashing-** Automation is being written to this control.
- **Green LED on**
  - ○ **If red LED is on**, Trim is active for this control.
  - ○ **If red LED is off**, Read or Trim + Read is active for this control.

- **Green LED flashing-** The control is in a Preview state.
- **Both LEDs off-** The automation for this control is not activated, or set to Off, and will not read or write automation.

It may help to see this status table turned around if you are wondering the state of a control:

Writing mode off	Red LED off	
Writing mode on:	Red LED on	
Automation currently writing:	Red LED Flashing	
Trim Mode on:		Green LED on.
Automation off or inactivated:	Red LED off	Green LED off
Preview state active	Red LED off	Green LED flashing

What Good Are Automation Mode Status LEDs?

When using Preview mode, a flashing green LED tells you that a control has been touched and its current state is part of the Preview Punch buffer. This can be extremely helpful if you think you *may* have accidentally touched a control which you do not want to change. It also confirms for you that you *have* touched a control which you do want to change. Great!

The other hobo signs here are not as exciting. They do tell you if automation is enabled, writing or not working at all, so if you do not see any LEDs lit on the controls you are working, stop and check the status.

Cascading Outputs

This is so obscure that I cannot find a reference to it in any of the Avid documentation. Here is a fast way to assign contiguous outputs to contiguous tracks.

For example, if you have ten tracks in your Pro Tools session and you want to assign them to outputs 1–10, the slow way is to go through them, one at a time, and assign each one. There is an easier way.

To cascade output assignments to selected tracks:

1. Assure that the desired output paths have been created (in **Setup > I/O...**).
2. Assure that the Audio Path Selector is visible in the Pro Tools window in which you are working.

3. Select all tracks which you want to assign to outputs. They do not need to be contiguous tracks, but they will be assigned to outputs in track order.
4. **Shift + Control + Command** – Click on the Audio Output Path Selector and select the first output path that you want to assign.

The selected tracks will be assigned to sequential outputs, beginning with the first selected.

If there are more tracks than output paths in your I/O, outputs will cycle back to the first selected and continue until all tracks are assigned.

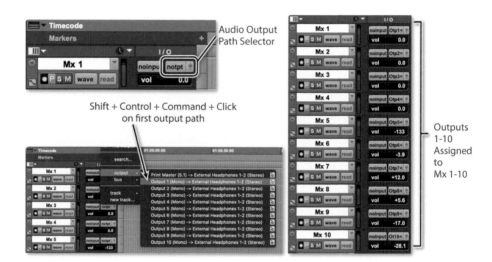

Cascade outputs

To cascade output assignments to *all* the tracks in the session (not recommended):

Use the above instructions, but at #4, don't use **Shift**. Instead, **Control + Command** and click on the Audio Output Path Selector.

This will ruin most mixing templates.

Reconfiguring Transport Keys
Is this the only way transport keys can be configured?

To quote Yoda: "There is another."

Yes, you *can* remap the Transport Keys!

This is one of those changes to the surface that you should do only with the involvement and approval of the studio engineer and in consultation with other console users.

Rearranging of the *functions* of the keys is done through the Soft Keys edit page, but it leaves the key caps indicating the wrong functions– which is never a good idea.

The key caps can be removed and reassembled into a different order, but this requires disassembling the Automation Module, which may void any warranties or get you banned from the studio. Keys cannot be rearranged without opening up the module, and most of us do not want to do that casually or frequently. Do not try prying them out, as they will break.

My advice is: do not remap functions without moving the keys to match, and do not consider opening the module case yourself. Get the studio engineer to do it. If you cannot convince the engineer that this is worthwhile, then do not do it.

Devil that I am, I cannot resist supplying a proposed alternate remapping which would make the Transport Keys much more friendly.

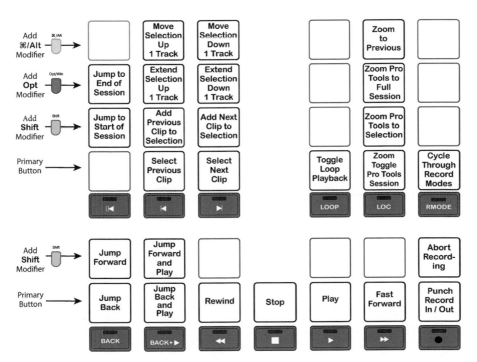

Alternative transport key remapping

Troubleshooting
Workstation Not Connecting to the S6 Surface

After starting up the workstation (the Mac), an application called WSControl should start up and connect Pro Tools to the S6.

Mac menu bar

While WSControl is searching, its icon in the Mac's menu bar will spin. Once the S6 has connected to the workstation it will stop spinning.

If the icon does not appear or does not stop spinning, try the following:

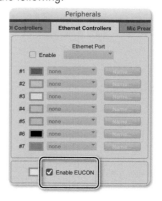

1. In Pro Tools, go to **Setup > Peripherals > Ethernet Controllers**.
2. Confirm that **Enable EUCON** is checked ON. If not, check it ON.
3. Shut down Pro Tools.
4. Restart the Mac.

If the system still does not link, there is little else that you can do yourself. Do not attempt further trouble-shooting!! Call your engineering team.

Pro Tools: peripherals window

Searching the Bank – Tracks Not Showing Up on the Surface

If your tracks do not display on the surface, they could be banked so that they are hidden, or the surface may be set to Layout Mode. Try one of these actions:

- **Tracks are banked off the surface**.
  Press the **User 1** Modifier key at the bottom of any fader module. Press it several times. If that does not work, press **User 2** even more times. If the surface suddenly populates with your tracks, use the banking keys to display the desired tracks on the surface. *Remember* that when you bank, you are moving the *window,* not the tracks, so directions may be reversed from your expectation *(see "Get Into Banking" on page 53 for more banking options).*

Modifier keys for banking

- **Layout Mode is active**.
  Check on the Lower Master Module, in the upper left button cluster. If the **Layout Mode** button is lit, press **mmShift + Layout Mode**. Leave the button unlit.

De-activate Layout Mode

- **One or more Spill Zones are active.**

  Hold **mmShift** and press any lit Spill buttons to de-activate spill.

De-activate Spill Zones

Not Hearing Any Audio When System Is Playing

There are too many reasons for this to happen to make a truly helpful list, but here are a few to check on the S6.

Check that Main speakers are selected in the Monitor section of the surface.

If using a Master Post Module, check the position of the Input/Playback paddles.

Audio Levels in the Mix Room Are Very Low

There are several common reasons. Here are three.

Reason	Solution
Dim is active.	Check Dim button on the Studio/Talk section of the Lower Master Module, bottom-right.
Monitor level has been turned down.	Check the main volume setting on the Studio/Talk section of the Lower Master Module, bottom-right.
Talkback or Listenback are active.	Check the Coms and Talk buttons on the Monitoring Controls section of the Lower Master Module, bottom-right. If either is lit, press and hold for one second to de-activate.

Modules Not Working

If modules seem to be powered but empty of tracks, see "Searching the Bank" on page 205.

Sometimes, modules will go on the blink. There are a few things to do to attempt to get them working again.

Go to **Settings** > **Surface/Config** on the Touchscreen.

The surface image will give you status of each module.

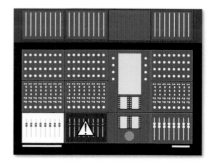

Surface config. image

Touch a module icon on the surface image to select it and display information about that module.

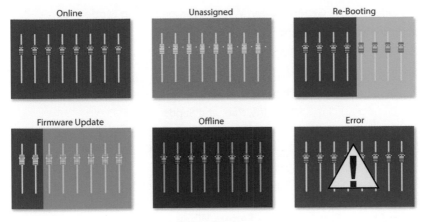

Module status icons

Things to try – in this order:

1. Reboot any troubled modules.
2. Power Cycle the S6.
3. Check that all modules and workstation have IP addresses in the same range.
4. Full Power cycle the S6 (shut down and turn off power).
   DO NOT DO THIS STEP ON YOUR OWN! Call your engineering support team.

Settings to Drive You Crazy

This section is not so much troubleshooting, as it is identifying and changing settings which are causing aggravation.

Session Taking a Long Time to Open

Uncheck this user setting: **Settings >User > Surface > Knobs /**

☐ **Pre-Load All Knobs on Session Load (Speeds Up All Mode)**

This will make the opening of sessions faster but may add time while mixing.

Plug-in and other windows continually pop up on the Pro Tools screen

These can be affected by the following settings:

- **Workstation > General/Workstation Follows Knob Set Changes**
- **Workstation > General/Open Windows on Knob Touch**
- **Workstation > General/Open Windows on Workstation Attention**

- Workstation > General/Open Windows when Editing Mode
  [Pulldown Menu]   -Off
  -Plug-Ins Only
  -Plug-Ins and Pan
  -Plug-Ins and Sends
  -Plug-Ins, Pan, and Sends

Plug-Ins Always Expand to the Knob Module When Selected

That function is set to Auto Expand.

- See **User > Surface > Strips > Auto Expand Functions**.

Plug-Ins Always Expand to the Faders When Selected

That function is set to Auto Expand faders.

- See **User > Surface > Strips > Auto Expand Faders**.

Talkback or Listenback remain active

Try one of these:

- On the Control Room area of the Lower Master Module, press and hold **Coms** and/or Talk button for one second.
- Go to **Monitoring Screen/Local Settings (✿)**.
  - Uncheck Auto Listenback and/or Auto Talkback.

Details of Example in Chapter 9

Track Name	Dx 1–10	Dx Vb1	Dx Vb2	Dx Sub	Dx Stem Record	PM Record
Track Type	Audio	Aux	Aux	Aux	Audio	Audio
Channels	Mono	5.0	5.0	5.1	5.1	5.1
Purpose	Dialog Source Level and processing on each track	Dx Reverb 1	Dx Reverb 2	Leveling and apply processing across all dialog tracks	Record and playback Dx Stem	Record and playback Printmaster
Insert 1*	7b EQ3*	Revibe II*	Revibe II*	Compressor Expander*	Insight Meter *	Insight Meter *
Insert 2*	McDSP SA2	–	–	McDSP NF575	–	–
Send1	Dx Vb 1	–	–	–	–	–
Send2	Dx Vb 2	–	–	–	–	–

Track Name	Dx 1–10	Dx Vb1	Dx Vb2	Dx Sub	Dx Stem Record	PM Record
Input	none	Dx Vb 1	Dx Vb 2	Dx Mix Bus	Dx Stem Bus	PM Rec Bus
Output	Dx Mix Bus	Dx Mix Bus	Dx Mix Bus	Dx Stem Bus	PM Rec Bus	Studio Output
* Specific processes are mixer's choice						

Default Location of Settings Files

As mentioned earlier, the S6 software allows you to save Title and Preference files, but it does not give you a way to delete them. With multiple users, or even with normal usage, the saved preference and title files can pile up and clutter the default directory.

To manage setting files on the S6 computer, you must log out of the S6 application and log in as an Administrator on the S6 computer. Using Windows Explorer, navigate to the default directories. There you can Cut, Copy, Rename, or Delete files in the Windows environment.

Some directories that you are seeking may be hidden, so when Window Explorers opens, select VIEW in the upper window. Set "Hidden items" to ON.

Since this is a Windows computer, there are a few tricks to using it that may not be obvious to Mac users.

To achieve a right-click on the touchscreen without a mouse, you must touch and hold an object until you see a small rectangle appear around your touch-point. Let go and the contextual menu will open.

(See "Outboard Keyboard" on page 10 for an alternative to poking at the touchscreen.)

Location of Files

Different references that I have seen have given different information about the location of Title and Preference files.

On the two S6 systems to which I have access, the default preference locations differ.

According to Avid, the S6 stores data files like this:

Layouts/Titles	C:\ProgramData\Avid\S6\Titles\
S6 System Preferences	C:\ProgramData\Avid\S6\
S6 User Preferences	C:\Users\S6User\AppData\Local\Avid\S6
SoftKeys	C:\ProgramData\Avid\S6\AppSets\
Default App	C:\ProgramData\Avid\S6\Appsets\

User preference files were found at:

C:\Users\Administrator\AppData\Local\Avid\S6

C:\Users\s6User\AppData\Local\Avid\S6

To locate the default preference file directory on your system:

Within S6 software:

1. Navigate Touchscreen to **Settings > User**.
2. Touch **Save**.
3. When the Explorer window opens, its search box shows the path of the default directory.
4. If the path name is truncated, click in the white space to the right of the truncated name and it will de–truncate.
5. If necessary, drag open the width of the window.
6. Make a note of this location.

To locate the default title file directory on your system:
Within S6 software:

1. Navigate Touchscreen to the Tracks page (shortcut: **mmShift + Tracks** on the Master Module).
2. Touch **Save** or **Load**.
3. Follow instructions 3–5 above.

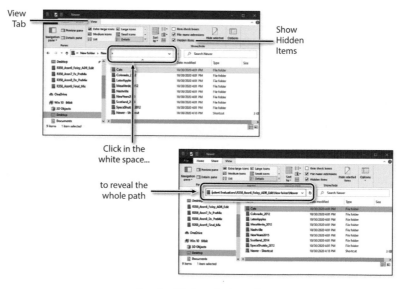

Revealing Windows directory paths

Appendix 2

System Settings – User Preferences

Listing of System Settings

System – General

▼ Preferences
Auto-Load from Titles and Sessions

□ User Preferences   □ Expand Faders

□ Banking/Layout State   □ Post Module State

□ Layouts and Meters   □ Post Layouts

□ Spill Zone State   □ Locked Strips State

□ Layout Banked Position

□ Merge Recalled Expand Faders with Current Faders[1]

System – Surface

▼ Brightness

□ Auto

Touchscreen

(Slider 10%–100%)

OLED, LED, Display Module

(Slider 10%–100%)

Console Timeout

(Slider 1min–2hrs)

□ Activate Screening Mode (Touch Master Module Screen to Exit)

---

1. When enabled, existing fader maps are not changed. Only new fader maps are imported. When disabled, existing fader maps will be replaced and new fader maps imported.

▼ **Strips**

☐ Disable Faders

▼ **GPIO**

☐ Talkback Enabled
☐ Monitoring Enabled (Dim, Cut)
☐ Transport Enabled (Stop, Play, Record)
Fader Start Glide Time (Slider 0–3 secs)
Fader Start Target (Slider – inf dB to +12 dB)

▼ **Language**

Track names language preference (requires application restart):
[Pulldown Menu]

System – Workstation

General
☐ Show Workstation Alerts
KVM Switch
☐ Support Enabled

KVM (Only visible when "Support Enabled" (above) is checked ON)

Listing of User Preferences

User – Surface

▼ Banking

Mode
  ☐ 8 Strips
  ☐ Whole Surface
Auto-Bank to Selected Track Mode
  ☐ Off
  ☐ If Not Visible on Surface
  ☐ Always
Banking Justification Mode
  Left/Right
Spill Left and Spill Right Justification Modes
  Left/Right   Left/Right

▼ Attention

Attention Most Recently Clicked DAW area
  ☐ Track Name   ☐ Fader   ☐ Edit Window
  ☐ Plug-Ins   ☐ Pan Controls   ☐ Sends
  ☐ Edit Selection Move Up/Down

Display Knobs from Most Recently Clicked DAW Area
  [Pulldown Menu]

  ☐ Attention Most Recently Selected Track (Legacy/Pro Tools 18,10, or Earlier)
  ☐ Select Most Recently Attentioned Track
  ☐ Attention Track of Most Recently Selected Surface Function
  ☐ Attention Track of Most Recently Selected Solo
  ☐ Focus Workstation of Most Recently Attentioned Track
  ☐ Show Home Screen on Strip Attention
Automatic Spill of Attentioned VCA
  [Pulldown menu] Off/Left of Attn Trk Fader/Right of Attn Trk Fader/ Left Spill Zone/Right Spill Zone

▼ **Strips**

Channel Selection Mode
- ○ Sum
- ⊙ Inter-Cancel

Solo Switch
- ○ Sum
- ⊙ Inter-Cancel
- ○ DAW Controlled

☐ Show Track Number
☐ Show Workstation Number
☐ Show Timed Fader Values

Fader Value Timeout

(Slider Off to 5 seconds)

☐ Bank Around Locked Strips – Banking Mode
☐ Bank Around Locked Strips – Layout Mode
☐ Show Hidden Tracks in Banking Mode
☐ Show Hidden Tracks in Layout Mode
☐ Show Hidden Tracks in VCA Spill
☐ Use Pro Tools Tracks Record Mode Colors
☐ Auto-Collapse Spill Zones With Layout Recall

Spill Zone Menu Key Mode for Layouts, Workstations or Types

(Pulldown)   LED's On

LEDs Off

LEDs On and Collapse Spill

Auto-Expand Functions

☐ Bus	☐ Group	☐ Pan
☐ Dynamics	☐ Heat	☐ Sends
☐ Edit	☐ Input	☐ Quick Controls
☐ EQ	☐ Inserts	
☐ Filters	☐ Instruments	☐ Auto-Expand Faders

▼ **Joystick Strips**

Assign Right Joystick Timeout
         (Slider Off – 3 Seconds)

User – Layouts

☐ Ignore Functions on Layout Recall

Layout Banked Position on Recall Mode
         [Pulldown Menu]

Auto-Save Changed Layout on Recall Mode
         [Pulldown Menu]

User – Knobs

☐ Send/Insert/Input Knobs Reversed

☐ Reverse Function Pages for 5-Knob Strips

☐ Remember Joystick Knobs by Track

Knob Maximum Speed (Default = 20)
         (Slider Slow – Fast)

Knob Sensitivity (Default = 30)
         (Slider Fine – Course)

Pan Knob Maximum Speed (Default = 65)
         (Slider Slow-Fast)

Pan Knob Sensitivity (Default = 52)
         (Slider Fine – Course)

Number of Knobs per Plug-In or Instrument Transmitted Over EUCON
         (Slider 100 – Unlimited)

☐ Pre-Load All Knobs on Session Load (Speeds Up All Mode)

User – Soft Keys

☐ Soft Key LEDs Enabled
☐ System Soft Key Icons Enabled
System Soft Key Display Mode (Pulldown)
  – Both Master Module Soft Key Displays
  – Left Master Module Soft Key Display Only
  – Right Master Module Soft Key Display Only
  – Both Automation Module Soft Key Displays
  – Left Automation Module Soft Key Displays
  – Right Automation Module Soft Key Displays
☐ Auto-Close Surface Recall Soft Keys

User – 3-D Panner

☐ Use 3-D Panner on Joystick Module
3D Panner Ceiling/Floor Rotation
    (Slider -90–90)
3D Panner Left/Right Rotation
    (Slider -90–90)

User – Workstation

▼ General

☐ Workstation Follows Knob Set Changes
☐ Open Windows on Knob Touch
☐ Open Windows on Workstation Attention

Open Windows when Editing Mode
    [Pulldown Menu]
☐ Close Windows When No Longer Editing
☐ Post Module Sends Record with Arm

▼ Solo

Mode

⊙ Solo in Place

⊙ After-Fader Listen

⊙ Pre-Fader Listen

User – Display Module

Common

☐ Show Automation

☐ Reverse Automation Lanes

Automation Opacity

(Slider 0%–100%)

Display

Layout (Pulldown)

Large Meters

Large Waveforms

Meters and Waveforms

Meters and Function. This is the System default display mode.

Waveforms and Function

Waveforms and Dual Functions

Waveforms and Dual Functions + Route

Waveform Zoom

(Slider 1 sec–60 sec)

Panner Divergence and Position Display Mode (Pulldown)

Left

Right

Both

Master Meter Display

Waveform Zoom

(Slider 1 sec–1 min)

Surface

(Opens Surface Configuration and Diagnostic Info window)

Local Options (⚙)

Home Screen – Local Options

☐ Attention Tracks from Meter Scroller
☐ Display Selection/Attentioned Track Border on Meter Scroller
☐ Track Scroller Follows Attentioned Track
☐ Link Meter Scroller to Track Scroller
Knob View
  ○ All Functions
  ⊙ Selected Functions
☐ Enable Attention Expand Knob Zone
☐ Enable Attention Expand Fader Zone
Open Plug-ins on Workstation When Knobs Assigned
  [Pulldown Menu]
  Master Module   Expand Fader Module
                                         1st Expand Knob Module
                                         2nd Expand Knob Module
1st Exp Knob Func and Backup Func Selected on Attn Change
  (2 Pulldowns)
           EQ   Bus
2nd Exp Knob Func and Backup Func Selected on Attn Change
  (2 Pulldowns)
           Dynamics   Last Selected
Expand Fader Function and Backup Func Selected on Attn Change
  (2 Pulldowns)
           Insert 1   Insert 2
Function and Knob Page Selected on Attention Change
  (2 Pulldowns)
           Last Selected   Last Selected
Backup Function and Knob Page Selected on Attention Change
           Pan   1st
☐ Auto-Show Function Graph on Selection.
Auto Show Function Graph on Knob Touch
  (Slider Off to 5.00 secs)

Tracks Screen – Local Options

▼ **Track Selector**

Position

   ○ Always Start with Channel 1 on All Page

   ○ Last position of Track Selector

   ⊙ Attentioned Track

☐ Display Breaks on Track Color

☐ Auto-Bank to Attentioned Track

☐ Show Home Screen on Track Attention

☐ Auto-Select Joystick Strips when Storing Layouts

☐ Store Hidden Virtual Strips in Layouts

☐ Double-Tap Assign to Copy Tracks from Banking Mode to Current Layout

Number of Strips in Layout

   (Slider 16–256)

▼ **Post Layouts**

Number of Post Strips in Post Layout

   (Slider 10–80)

☐ Mirror Post Strips on Multiple Post Modules

▼ **Meter Layouts**

Layout (Pulldown)

   (7 Meter Layouts)

Number of Meter Rows

   (Slider 1–4)

Monitoring Screen – Local Options

▼ **Workstation**

☐ Show Custom Name in Available List.

Surface Config Screen – Local Options

▼ **Surface**

Desk ID (changes require restart)

(Slider 1–30)

▼ **Network Interfaces (changes require system shut down)**

Network Interface 1 IP Setting (Intel ® 82579LM Gigabit Network Connection)

(Pulldown)

☐ Enable DHCP Server on Interface 1

Network Interface 2 IP Setting (Intel ® 82579LM Gigabit Network Connection)

(Pulldown)

☐ Enable DHCP Server on Interface 2

Appendix 3

Button Names Lookup

Button Functions of the Master Modules (by Button Name)

Button Name	Location	Action
Plus (+) + amShift	Automation Module Jog Wheel Section	Behaves same as **Trim** button (below).
Plus (+) or Minus (−)	Automation Module Jog Wheel Section	Does nothing by itself.
Plus (+) or Minus (−) + Opt/Win	Automation Module Jog Wheel Section	Applies a fade in (-) or fade out (+) from the insertion point to the end of selected clips starting from the insertion point.
Plus (+) or Minus (−) + amShift	Automation Module Jog Wheel Section	Trims the head (-) or tail (+) of selected clips to the insertion point.
Plus (+) or Minus (−) + Shift	Automation Module Jog Wheel Section	Also removes the head (-) or tail (+) of all clips to the insertion point.
Mixer (<) + mmShift	Master Module Navigation Section	Toggles the main PT window between Edit and Mix windows.
< or >	Master Module Navigation Section	Bank left or right by 1 strip.
<< or >>	Master Module Navigation Section	Banks surface or active Spill Zone left or right by 8 strips or whole surface, depending on settings (User > Surface > Banking > Mode).
Home (<<) or End (>>) + mmShift	Master Module Navigation Section	Banks surface or active Spill Zone to start or end.
Close (>) + mmShift	Master Module Navigation Section	Closes the frontmost main PT window, possibly closing both if used twice.
All	Master Module Navigation Section	Applies button presses in the Process section to all tracks when lit.

Button Name	Location	Action
Clear Clip	Master Module Navigation Section	Clears the clip lights across the surface.
Clear Solo	Master Module Navigation Section	Clears Solo state of all tracks of the session.
Consol Clip	Automation Module Locate Section	Applies Consolidate Clip command, rendering a file or files of selected clips (Alt name: **Store Locate**).
Coms	Lower Master Module Speaker Select area	Activates Listenback microphone.
Cut	Master Module Studio/ Talk	Mutes the control room monitor.
Dim	Master Module Studio/ Talk	Dims the control room monitor level by the dim amount.
Display 1 or **Display 2**	Master Module Navigation Section	Changes the scale of any waveform displays in Display Layouts.
Display 1 or **Display 2 + mmShift**	Master Module Navigation Section	Changes the Display Layout of all active displays.
Down Arrow (↓)	Automation Module Locate Section	Clears Selection and sets the current playhead location as the insertion point.
Down Arrow (↓) + Shift	Automation Module Locate Section	Resets the previous selection.
Edit Loc	Automation Module Locate Section	When active (flashing) selecting a Memory Location from the Soft Key pads will open the Memory Location Edit window instead of recalling the location itself (Alt Name: **Edit**).
Faders Off	Automation Module Locate Section	Disables all fader controls, only faders are affected (Alt name: **Trim**).
Flip	Master Module Navigation Section	Swaps control of functions with the volume fader. Press to cycle all parameters currently showing to the fader; **mmShift + Flip** to clear flip mode.

Button Name	Location	Action
Jog	Automation Module Jog Wheel Section	When active, turning the Jog Wheel scrubs the first 2 selected tracks.
L Spill or **R Spill**	Master Module Navigation Section	Readies that Spill Zone for assignment into Spill Zone.
Layout Mode	Master Module Navigation Section	Assigns Track Layouts to the master module Soft Key pads.
Layout Mode + mmShift	Master Module Navigation Section	Places surface into Layout Mode. **mmShift** again to leave Layout Mode.
Mark In	Automation Module Locate Section	Sets Mark In mode, where the In point of a Selection is shifted using the Jog Wheel.
Mark Out	Automation Module Locate Section	Sets Mark Out mode, where the Out point of a Selection is shifted using the Jog Wheel.
Mem Loc	Automation Module Locate Section	Assigns Memory Location Soft Key page 1 to the Automation Module Soft Key pad.
Mem Loc + Shift	Automation Module Locate Section	Assigns Memory Location Soft Key pages 1–4 to Soft Key pads.
Mix / Edit	Master Module Navigation Section	Toggles the Pro Tools display window between Mix and Edit. (Alt name: **Trim +**)
ReDo	Automation Module Locate Section	Re-does last un-done edit. (Alt name: **Delete**)
Save	Automation Module Locate Section	Saves the session when pressed twice in a row. (Alt name: **Clear**)
Save + Shift	Automation Module Locate Section	Opens **Save As...** dialog.
Shuttle	Automation Module Jog Wheel Section	When active, plays the first 2 selected tracks. Speed and direction controlled by the Jog Wheel.
Talk	Lower Master Module Speaker Select area	Activates Talkback microphone.

Button Name	Location	Action
Tracks	Master Module Navigation Section	Opens Tracks screen on the Touchscreen.
Trim	Automation Module Jog Wheel Section	When active, turning the Jog Wheel moves the edit selection forward or backward without playing. When Link Timeline and Edit Selection is active, insertion point moves as well.
Trim Sel	Automation Module Locate Section	Applies Trim Clip to Selection command, same as Command+T in Pro Tools. (Alt name: **Store Current**)
Type	Lower Master Module	Assigns Types to the Master Module Soft Key pads.
Undo	Automation Module Locate Section	Undoes last edit. (Alt name: **Recall**)
WS	Master Module Navigation Section	Assigns Workstation controls to Master Module Soft Key Pads.
WS + mmShift	Master Module Navigation Section	Opens Workstation screen on the Touchscreen.
Zoom Horizontal	Automation Module Jog Wheel Section	When active, the horizontal zoom of the Pro Tools window is adjusted.
Zoom Horizontal + amShift	Automation Module Jog Wheel Section	When active, the Jog Wheel scrolls the Pro Tools window horizontally.
Zoom Vertical	Automation Module Jog Wheel Section	When active, the height of all selected tracks is adjusted with the Jog Wheel.
Zoom Vertical + amShift	Automation Module Jog Wheel Section	When active, the Jog Wheel scrolls the Pro Tools window up or down.

Appendix 4

Soft Key Quick-Jump Shortcuts

Avid S6 Soft Key Page – Pro Tools App Set v2018.3

Press **Shift** (modifier key) + Character to assign Pro Tools pre-sets

Character	Name	Description	Note
Shift + 0	Default	The default Soft Key pages are shown in all banks.	**Automation 1 Session Management 1, Automation 2,** and **Extras 1.**
Shift + 1	Automation	All four banks of Soft Keys display Automation pages.	**Automation 1, 2, 3, 4**
Shift + 2	Automation Alt 1	Automation pages 1 and 2 appear on the Automation Module Soft Key Pads.	Useful when Layouts are shown in both the left and right Soft Key Pads.
Shift + 3	Automation Alt 2	Automation page 1 appears on the right Master Module Soft Key Pad.	Useful when Layouts are shown on only the left bank.
Shift + 4	Management	Session management pages appear on all banks.	Better done in Pro Tools.
Shift + 5	Satellites & Machines	All four banks display pages for Satellites, Machine Control, Solo (SIP/AFL/PFL, and switch behavior), and more.	Better done in Pro Tools.
Shift + 6	Configuration Editor	Interface, Tools and Setup, Session Management 1, and Counters & Scrolling pages appear on the four banks.	
Shift + 7	Editing	Pages and commands to edit Clips, Clip Gain, Clip FX, Selections, and Tracks.	Better done in Pro Tools.
Shift + 8	MIDI	MIDI composition, creation, and editing commands.	
Shift + 9	Recording	Commands for recording, tracking, and playlists.	
Shift + Enter	Spill Zones	Bank, Nudge, Home, and End for each Spill Zone (Left and Right).	
Shift + "." (decimal)	Control Room	Access all control room Sources and Speakers, toggle. Sum/Inter-cancel modes, access Fold-downs, Talkback and Listenback, and access Monitoring Preferences.	These pages give direct control of all banking.
Shift + /	User Pages	Places blank User Page 2 into lower-right Key Pad, gives access to User pages 1 and 3. Page 3 is nearly identical to Automation 2, but it has Save button.	
Shift + *	Preferences	Frequently used S6 Preference settings.	
Shift + Mem Loc	Memory Locations	All four Soft Key Pads allocated to Memory Locations.	

Avid S6 Soft Key Page - Pro Tools App Set v2019.5

Press **Shift** (modifier key) + Character to assign Pro Tools pre-sets

Character	Name	Description	Note
Shift + 0	Default	The default Soft Key pages are shown in all banks.	**Automation 1 Session Management 1, Automation 2,** and **Extras 1.**
Shift + 1	Automation	All four banks of Soft Keys display Automation pages.	**Automation 1, 2, 3, 4**
Shift + 2	Automation Alt 1	Automation pages 1 and 2 appear on the Automation Module Soft Key Pads.	Useful when Layouts are shown in both the left and right Soft Key Pads.
Shift + 3	Automation Alt 2	Automation page 1 appears on the right Master Module Soft Key Pad.	Useful when Layouts are shown on only the left bank.
Shift + 4	Management	Session management pages appear on all banks.	Better done in Pro Tools.
Shift + 5	Satellites & Machines	All four banks display pages for Satellites, Machine Control, Solo (SIP/AFL/PFL), and switch behavior), and more.	Better done in Pro Tools.
Shift + 6	Configuration Editor	Interface, Tools and Setup, Session Management 1, and Counters & Scrolling pages appear on the four banks.	
Shift + 7	Editing	Pages and commands to edit Clips, Clip Gain, Clip FX, Selections, and Tracks.	Better done in Pro Tools.
Shift + 8	MIDI	MIDI composition, creation, and editing commands.	
Shift + 9	Recording	Commands for recording, tracking, and playlists.	
Shift + Enter	Zone Banking	Bank, Nudge, Home, and End for each Spill Zone (Left and Right).	These pages give direct control of all banking.
Shift + "." (decimal)	Control Room	Access all control room Sources and Speakers, toggle. Sum/Inter-cancel modes, access Fold-downs, Talkback and Listenback, and access Monitoring Preferences.	
Shift + /	Track and Meter Layouts	Track Layouts, Meter Layouts.	
Shift + ★	Preferences	Console Preferences.	
Shift + Mem Loc	Memory Locations	Memory Locations in all Soft Key pads.	

Index

Image Index